hidden HUNGER

overcoming eating

disorders through God's

healing power

hidden HUNGER

Maxine Davies

Authentic
LIFESTYLE

08 07 06 05 04   7 6 5 4 3 2 1

First published 2004 by Authentic Lifestyle, an imprint of
Authentic Media, 9 Holdom Avenue, Bletchley, Milton Keynes,
MK1 1QR and
P.O. Box 1047, Waynesboro, GA 30830-2047, USA

British Library Cataloguing in Publication Data
A catalogue record for this book is available from the British
Library

1-86024-296-0

Cover design by David Lund
Printed in Denmark by Nørhaven

Dedication

I would like to dedicate this book to my mum. My mum is not only my mum but my friend as well. My mother has the most beautiful blue eyes, which really do reflect Jesus' love. My mum was the one to introduce me to Jesus when I was little and has encouraged and prayed for me ever since. Just want to say thank you, and I love you very much.

I would like to thank my family and friends, especially Shelley, for being such a wonderful friend to me, and I would also like to thank David and Charmaine Hicks for helping me to write this book, and for all their love and encouragment during my time in Toronto.

This book is a must-read for people who are struggling with eating disorders or know people who are struggling with eating disorders. It speaks very clearly about the underlying issues that cause eating disorders and how the wonderful love and power of our Heavenly father is able to bring healing to all those who struggle in this area.

Carol Arnott,
Toronto Airport Christian Fellowship

Hidden Hunger is written from Maxine's heart and reflects her personal experience of receiving and ministering the Father's love. I wholeheartedly recommend this book, not only for those suffering from an eating disorder, but also for anyone looking to depen their relationship with God.

Ze Markee
Folly's End Church

Contents

Foreword

*E*ating disorders are a rampant problem in today's society. There is much material available helping to diagnose but unfortunately few health professionals believe eating disorders can be truly cured. I believe, aside from God, they're probably right.

Hidden Hunger offers real hope to those who are struggling. Here you will find general and diagnostic information about these disorders but, more importantly, you will find spiritual insight into the root causes and keys to true and lasting freedom. Maxine treats this subject from both a personal and a godly perspective. With the compassion that comes from her own journey to freedom, Maxine shares from the word of God and her experience.

Whether you struggle yourself with an eating disorder, or suspect someone you love might, *Hidden Hunger* is a book I highly recommend. It offers real solutions to very real problems.

Shelley Duesbury (née Fortier)
Administrator and Counsellor, Prayer and Care
Department, TACF

Why Did You Pick Up This Book?

ood is personal. It touches on issues which are personal, even intimate – your likes and dislikes, comforts and cravings, family history, home life, and social life. So since this is a book about problems related to food, I'm going to begin with the assumption that you're reading this book for personal reasons.

Perhaps you're involved in church ministry and are interested in understanding food and weight problems from a ministry point of view

Or . . . you know someone who is having trouble controlling their weight or eating patterns, and you want to understand what is happening

Or . . . you're wondering if you're getting into trouble with your appetite (or lack of it) but aren't sure if it's really a problem;

Or . . . you *know* something's wrong, but you don't understand or know what to do about it.

This book is an expanded version of teaching I give in seminars and conferences, and I've called it *Hidden Hunger*. Why? Because I know that although eating problems are very real, they're actually the symptoms of a

I know that although eating problems are very real, they're actually the symptons of a much deeper hunger which is usually hidden

much deeper hunger which is usually hidden – even from those who are desperate to be free. And I've found that if you can understand the deeper longing, which is showing up in the area of food, then relief and freedom will come.

The world today seems to be obsessed with food and body image: eating disorders are becoming a huge problem especially in teenagers – it isn't really a hidden issue any more.

However . . .

In typical daily life, a person's struggles with their own food, appetite and weight are a very private (and usually quite a hidden) battle, filled with frustration, pain and despair. It may be even tougher in and around churches. Eating disorders aren't really spoken about in churches today.

I'm still amazed at the number of women who come to me when I speak somewhere and tell me they've been struggling for years but they've been too ashamed and embarrassed to tell anyone about what's been going on. They feel like complete spiritual failures.

Ministering to the bodies

If you stop and think about it, a lot of church life revolves around food: church social dinners, the annual picnic lunches, women's luncheons, men's breakfasts, youth group pig-outs . . . . There was a series of women's early breakfast meetings I used to go to and I must admit that it was definitely the homemade bread, sticky buns and fresh coffee that motivated me to get out of bed!

We all like to eat and to have a healthy appetite is a good thing.

More hunger than appetite

However, for many people I have spoken to, there is a deep hunger inside that eating food just doesn't seem to satisfy.

In fact, food can't reach deep enough. We keep hoping that the good feelings we get from food will make us feel better, happier. But food won't touch the real source of the hunger. (Alternatively, for the anorexic or compulsive dieter, we keep hoping that pushing food away will make us feel better inside – perhaps even a better person. But the same deep emptiness remains.)

And when you're having a bad day gripped in a tidal wave of sadness, or loneliness, or frustration, or confusion, and you reach for a carton of smooth, sweet, cooling, *innocent* ice cream, you tell yourself, 'This isn't so bad . . . this will make me feel better . . . I can deal with life later . . . (there's an instant gratification) right now I need this ice cream and chocolate bar, oh and this cake.' But the problem is: it never does satisfy.

You see it's not really about the food. Or even the calories. It's an emotional thing that's happening. And the physical feeling can put you in Ice Cream Heaven while you're polishing it off, and for a few minutes your problems don't seem so bad. But it wears off just as quickly and you're left feeling sick, disappointed and ashamed.

Or if you're anorexic, you too have had a bad day but instead of food being a comfort you deny yourself food and hope that the weight you're losing will satisfy you. But it doesn't – does it?

Something for everyone

Although I'm focusing on eating disorders, specifically bulimia, you will probably begin to read between the lines that the roots of these problems are universal, and actually relate to a wider range of hungers, drives and urges. Perhaps you don't struggle with under- or over-eating. Maybe you relate more to cravings for specific foods, such as chocolate, sweets, alcohol, coffee, tea, rich cream sauces, scorching chilli sauces, and so on. I'm not saying any of these are bad things. They can be just normal preferences and personal tastes. But they can also cross over into becoming unhealthy.

Or if foods don't do it for you, maybe you've found something else to use.

Like exercise: you're irritable if you don't get that 'runner's high'

Or . . . working on a new diet lifestyle programme: 'I heard this one works'

Or . . . shopping: what we call 'retail therapy'

Or . . . you immerse yourself in a time-and-energy-consuming ministry, career or business

Or . . . you're getting your buzz from adrenaline-pumping music.

There's no limit to the options at hand to soothe the discomforts or fill the voids in our lives. In these cases, people are usually compensating for something. And they don't even know they're feeding a hunger.

So whatever your original reason was for picking up this book, give God permission to speak to you about your life. Maybe you don't have an eating disorder, but you might find that he's just been waiting for you to get curious about it so he can minister to you about some other hunger!

So, where to begin?

The whole area of why something which is normal can get so out of control is a huge and bewildering issue. So, for this small book, I am focusing on struggles with eating and appetite. I don't intend this book to be an exhaustive medical and psychological study – there are lots of those books already and many do a good job of defining problems . . . but that won't usually change the problem. I want to go beyond describing and understanding, and get to the healing!

In order to get there, of course, I'll need to point out some facts and give you my personal observations. But we won't stop there. The goal of this book is to help you find your way out of your eating problems.

So I think it'll be helpful if we look at things in this order:

Basics: how professionals medically describe eating disorders.

Background: what could go on in someone's life to make them susceptible to food problems.

Beginning: how an eating disorder can get started.

Body behaviour: why food becomes so tangled with our emotions.

Battle in the mind: why it's such a struggle that rages in both your mind and body.

Breaking out: how the pain and confusion can be broken, so that freedom can begin.

Back to the roots: the kind of healing process one might go through with the Lord. (You'll understand later why I'm differentiating between an eating disorder being broken and being healed.)

And finally, I'll take you through some prayers and practical steps to start you on your way to your own healing . . . and you can read some testimonies that I'm sure will help and encourage you.

Who am I to be writing this?

By now you must be wondering who I am to be writing about such a mysterious and complicated problem. I suppose I'm a kind of expert because I've been healed of an eating disorder myself.

In my case, it was bulimia. And God showed me his love and his power by changing that part of me that was out of control. He broke the grip of my eating disorder. And since then he has stayed by me to walk me through the personal issues in my life which were driving my bulimia.

I'm not a medical specialist. But my own struggles motivated me to read about the medical aspects of food and food disorders.

The Lord has asked me to bring a message of hope and healing to people. (Which, believe me, is probably the last thing I thought I'd ever share in public – let alone teach on it!)

I'll give you a handful of interesting facts and figures about eating disorders but, as I said, there are lots of clinical books already out there. Most of what I am going to be sharing with you is my own story, some personal observations, and most importantly the things that God has taught me about my own experience which will help other people going through similar struggles. I believe the Lord has given me keys of understanding that will help you to unlock the traps and bondages you are experiencing in your own life.

Listen as you read

As I share my story, God might bring something to mind from your own life – insight will come to you and you'll think, 'Hmm, I haven't thought about that person in years.' Or: 'Oh! I wonder if that's important.' It might be someone's face, a memory from your life, a name, a place . . . even a dream. God will bring these things to the surface because he wants to help you through this. We just need to listen.

So when this happens, *please* write it down somewhere so you know you'll come back to it. Write it in the margin of the page you're reading, or in the back pages of this book, or in your personal journal. Whatever you do, don't just tell yourself that you'll remember later. You won't, so write it down!

Before you go on reading, take just a moment to ask the Lord to speak to you personally, into your thoughts, to help you realise what's been going on. And tell him you don't want to ignore what he shows you.

If you're not sure what to say, try this:

Lord, I want all the help you can give me to understand what's going on. I give you permission to speak into my thoughts and memories about what's important, and keep the other stuff back for now. Thanks for caring.

Maybe you are reading this book and don't know God but that's OK! He knows you and wants to help you through this. So why not give him a chance? You've tried everything else. There comes a point in life where you have to choose to give your life to Jesus – or not. My prayer is that you will, and in doing so, will find out what a wonderful friend he is.

1

Basics

edically, food disorders fall into three cate
gories: anorexia nervosa, bulimia, and compulsive eating.

Anorexia nervosa

Anorexia is usually defined as a deliberate and excessive
starvation in the pursuit of thinness. Now if you were to
go to a doctor, this is what he or she would look for before
saying, 'Yes, this is a medical problem.'

- If your body weight is at least 15 per cent under what
  is normal for your age and height – so if you should be
  115 lb., but weigh 98 lb. or less).
- In females, missing at least three consecutive menstrual
  cycles.
- There's an intense fear of gaining weight or becoming fat
  – even when clearly underweight by objective standards.
- There is a disturbance in the way one's own body
  weight, size or shape is visually perceived and men-
  tally experienced – an anorexic person will often say, 'I
  feel fat, I feel ugly, I feel horrible . . . I just *feel* really fat!'
  even though they are very, very thin. They can even

look at someone else who is thin and recognise that the person is seriously underweight – but not see this when they look at themselves. This is a difficult thing to understand, but when anorexia gets a hold of a woman, she can stand in front of a mirror and look at herself, and yet not be able to see that she's thin – she will actually think and feel that she's fat. It isn't logical; so don't expect it to be. More on this later.

Bulimia

This is a pattern of recurring episodes of swinging between binge eating – which means eating lots of food in a short space of time, and forced elimination – which means making yourself sick.

- The person feels driven to comfort or satisfy herself by eating large amounts of food in a short time, followed by a feeling of lack of self-control.
- Then, there's a swing to feelings of guilt and, wanting to compensate somehow, the person forces herself to get rid of the food – often by self-induced vomiting, or the use of laxatives or diuretics, or some combination.
- As with anorexia, there is a persistent over-concern with body shape and weight.

Compulsive over-eating

More than the occasional over-indulgence, this is an uncontrollable consumption of large amounts of food *not based on hunger*.

- You can't resist eating something and feel driven while eating, as if you can never get enough food.

- You are always hungry, even if you've just eaten.

It's quite common for people with an eating disorder to find themselves struggling with all three at different times

Now these three different categories share some traits and can overlap in a person's experience. It's quite common for people with an eating disorder to find themselves struggling with all three at different times. It all kind of mixes together, I think, because the root causes are shared.

So, for instance, somebody who is coming out of anorexia can fall into a pattern of bulimia because they rationalise that at least they're eating. Or if they're being pressured to eat by family or friends, they may find ways to get rid of the food privately. Or a bulimic person may try to cope or break the pattern by refusing to eat at all.

It's the same with bulimia and compulsive over-eating, since both often involve craving the satisfaction of eating food. One difference is that the bulimic person is often obsessed with becoming thin while the compulsive over-eater is desperate for the comfort of eating. But I've had a lot of women come to me who over-eat and admit that the only reason they aren't bulimic is that the vomiting was just too horrible for them to go through with – I tell them to thank God they couldn't do it.

As you might imagine, the lines between these categories of eating problems can get fuzzy because people's experiences are so different, and people often go back and forth between these behaviours.

Think about it.

- When an anorexic person withholds food from their body, it obviously isn't because their thin little body doesn't need the nourishment.
- Someone who is bulimic doesn't make themselves sick because it's part of enjoying a meal.
- A compulsive over-eater doesn't keep pushing down more food because their body actually needs it, or just because it tastes good. Something in that person's thinking is driving them – usually something in their personal background.

So there's no point in telling someone with a food problem to just stop doing what they're doing. There are root causes to eating disorders and reasons behind the things we do to try to smooth things over and push down the pain.

2

Background

So what could set someone up to fall into such a strange and painful state? In truth, the factors and combinations of factors are as varied as people's individual personalities and personal histories. But there are common themes for most people. In my own case, several aspects of my background combined to set me up for bulimia. So I'm going to use my personal experience to illustrate.

Just about everyone struggles to some degree with loving and accepting themselves

Insecurities and bad self-image

Just about everyone struggles to some degree with loving and accepting themselves, but for people struggling with eating disorders we aren't talking about an occasional bout of inferiority; it feels like a never-ending battle you cannot win. A woman with an eating disorder may try a number of different ways of coping.

- Talking herself into adopting a positive outlook, 'speaking out positively, I am beautiful'.
- Joking about herself in order to give the impression that she doesn't take herself (or her problems) too seriously.
- Becoming socially pleasing, making sure she's fun to be around, the old 'jolly fat person' cliché.
- Building a role as a burden bearer – a sympathetic person who's known for carrying others and their problems, either emotionally, practically or financially.
- Or simply choosing to ignore things: keep smiling and carry on!

These strategies can work for a while, but it takes constant effort to maintain that kind of control in public if underneath you just feel alone and defeated. The susceptible person finds they are too often crying themselves to sleep, or becoming progressively more resigned to being sad or depressed. Even if they are coping on the outside, on the inside they are profoundly unhappy.

And for the woman with an eating disorder, what we're usually talking about is a deep dissatisfaction with herself – most often with the way her body looks.

Now before you jump to any conclusions about these people, I'm not talking about someone who you'd call vain because she's just so pleased with what she sees in the mirror. This is someone who *despises* the way she looks, she's completely unhappy and discouraged with her appearance and feels defeated by it.

This is me ...

In my own case, this started fairly early. Here's my artistic impression of what I thought of myself when I was twelve years old.

You can see a number of interesting features here. Basically, all the things I didn't like about myself.

For instance, something that I absolutely hated was my hair. You wouldn't guess from looking at me now, but it was dead straight until I was about twelve. Then I guess hormones or whatever kicked in and my hair started to get very curly. And naturally, as a pre-teen girl, what I had was exactly what I didn't want.

I desperately wanted to have a fringe (or 'bangs' as they say in North America) so I taped my hair to my forehead every night when I went to bed. But every morning when I woke up, *boing*! It bounced right back up. And I hated it.

To make matters worse, I used to cycle to school through the damp autumn air, so by the time I got to school, my curly fringe was way up near the top of my head and stood out like a fuzzy golden halo that framed my face. I would desperately try to pull it into shape before meeting my friends.

Most nights, my prayer life consisted of my desperate pleas to the Lord to change my hair.

Next, did you find while growing up, that parts of your face grew before others – maybe your lips, or ears, or cheeks? For a while it seems like you are all out of proportion and out of shape. Well, my nose decided to venture out and make a life for itself before the rest of my face caught on. I was very self-conscious about my nose and I was forever looking in the mirror trying to squash it down a bit, hoping I could get it to stay in a little.

What made it worse was that my dad had a teasing kind of sense of humour, and he thought it was funny to walk past me and pretend he had cut the back of his hand on the end of my nose. But to a young girl who was already insecure about the way she looked, it was not helpful humour.

I also blushed a lot. I would go very red, very easily. In fact, just putting my hand up in class to answer a question made me turn scarlet! And there was nothing I could do to hide it. So I made sure I kept quiet.

I hated that I blushed and used to wish I had dark skin – that way nobody would know.

And then there was the teasing. There was a group of boys at my school who decided that I was an easy target to make fun of. If they weren't teasing me about my hair it was about my going red. So of course I inevitably turned even redder! And then they'd lick a fingertip, touch my forehead and go, 'Tsss!' as if they'd burned themselves. Seems funny now but at the time it wasn't. I hated going to school. And the boys were the worst part.

So by the age of twelve, I pretty much hated myself and had very little confidence.

One of my sister Maria's fondest memories of me while growing up is of me standing in front of the bathroom mirror, Sellotape in my hair, squashing down my nose, moaning and complaining about how I looked, while she was busily dental-flossing her teeth.

I remember that I actually hated looking in the mirror. When all the other girls were fussing with their hair in the girls' room, I avoided the mirror. I mean I *really* despised myself. I was desperate for some reassurance.

A bad self-image is fertile ground for other problems to take root

My sisters used to laugh at me and figure I would get over it someday.

Don't we 'get over it'?

I can just hear you wondering, 'But isn't this kind of thing just normal? I mean, who gets through childhood without that?' True, these are common experiences, and I'm not saying that everyone who gets teased is going to develop an eating disorder, but a bad self-image is fertile ground for other problems to take root.

The Scriptures say, 'Reckless words pierce like a sword' (Prov. 12:18). No doubt, you've felt that, and this can be the beginning for a lot of children who later develop an eating disorder. They hear a lot of words that wound so deeply, and they don't receive the care or understanding that they need to develop the resilience to cope with the effect of those hurtful words. They need the comfort, wisdom and encouragement of a father, mother, grand-parent, or even older brothers and sisters.

Remember, you're now looking back at those experiences from the perspective of an adult, so it's easier to intellectu-alise it all and shrug it off because there are more 'impor-tant', rational, grown-up things to think about other than what someone said about your ears! But children have this wonderful way of living life 'in the moment'. So to the child going through it, this *is* life – it's the only life they know. Right now you're looking back on it, but back then you lived it. And that's when so much of the damage is done.

Think about your own experience: in all likelihood, you had cutting words aimed and fired at you, and you found some of it believable, and you wound up agreeing. Your agreement gave those words power over your way of viewing and thinking about things, i.e. what you were willing to accept as 'just the way things are', or 'growing pains', or even 'normal childhood'. Being resigned to it all probably took those pains (sadness, anger, pessimism, etc.) and cemented them in place as part of your normal life.

This happened to me. So as a young girl about to enter my teenage years this was not very good preparation.

The losing battle of comparison

Like everyone else, I compared myself to others. You know how you are in school and you start to do the comparing thing: can I fit in, do I measure up, can I get a boyfriend, who would choose me? At the same time, as a teenager you start looking for clues and advice about what you can do to be more adult, and you scan for attractive examples of what to be like.

We have a situation in the West where our insecurities about our personal image are fanned into flame by the mass media

Usually, it's mostly about how we look to others. We want someone to help us, to tell us what to do, so it'll turn out OK.

If we're fortunate, we'll get healthy, helpful input about our image at home. But so often it's either left unsaid, or isn't there at all. Or we turn outward and deliberately choose outside ideas and standards. And there are multi-billion pound industries just waiting to help us do that.

Now I'm not going to just bash the media simply because it's a big, obvious, easy target. Yet while we may not be able to say these sources and examples *cause* insecurities, we have a situation in the West (and countries influenced by western culture) where our insecurities about our personal image are fanned into flame by the mass media. Because in the media, image is everything! Have you ever watched a romantic comedy believing you have to have a body like a gorgeous film star to get the man? Or spent an afternoon looking through a magazine only to be left feeling quite depressed by all the stunning models smiling back at you?

Big companies know why they are spending thousands of pounds on a photograph, hundreds of thousands to print or broadcast an ad, and millions on a marketing campaign in order to influence how we spend our money: buy this, eat this, and you'll look and feel wonderful! They're not out to hypnotise or brainwash us: all they have to do is draw the eye so we'll reach a couple of inches further down the shelf to where their product sits.

The meaning of life

And so much of it comes down to body image. It's not difficult to see what society communicates through TV and the other media: that the single most important role for a woman today is to look beautiful and be attractive. Some men experience this too, but I think it's more blatant for women. If we are beautiful, then we will be successful, wanted, chosen and loved.

And the key thing here relating to anorexia, bulimia, and even compulsive over-eating, is that we are told over and over again this basic, self-evident truth:

To be attractive, thou shalt be thin!

I was reading a magazine article in the *National Enquirer* (27 October 1998) which talked about 'starving stars' diet torture', pointing out how women were losing their jobs in Hollywood because they were at a normal body weight and media directors were demanding thinner bodies. There was to be a big court case as to whether you could actually be fired for being at a normal body weight.

And we often forget that it wasn't always this way. It's only been in the last one or two centuries (out of the last fifty or sixty) that we've become so obsessed with being thin, even gaunt. It used to be that body fat was widely accepted or admired – partly because it signified that you were healthy and rich enough to eat well, but it was also thought of as beautiful to have curves and be a bit rounded.

And even now, in many parts of the world extra body fat is easily accepted. I know in Costa Rica, Central America, calling a woman friend *Gorda* (Spanish for 'Chubby') is not offensive.

But often, people who naturally carry perfectly healthy amounts of body fat are teased as children, and then as adults they're relentlessly told that they aren't acceptable. The media says, 'This is what the perfect woman or perfect man looks like. So if you don't look like this then there's a problem.'

Well, I wanted to look like the girls on TV

Am I exaggerating?

I have spoken on eating disorders in high schools and it's so easy to see that these teenage girls are as thin as thin can be. And they are watching music videos and being convinced that thin is sexy and attractive. While the role models get thinner and thinner and skinnier and skinnier so do the girls who watch them. I spoke to an eleven-year-old girl who said she had been anorexic since she was eight years old. When I asked her why, she said: 'Well, I wanted to look like the girls on TV.'

Are these pressures imagined or real?

Here are some numbers to think about:

- In the UK, nearly 2 in every 100 secondary school girls suffer from anorexia, bulimia nervosa or binge-eating disorder.
- A 1998 survey done by Exeter University included 37,500 young women between twelve and fifteen. Over half (57 per cent) listed appearance as the biggest concern in their lives. The same study indicated that 59 per cent of the twelve- and thirteen-year-old girls who suffered from low self-esteem were also dieting.
- In the United States, The National Association of Anorexia Nervosa and Associated Disorders reports that seven million American women and almost two million men suffer from eating disorders, including children.
- The US Public Health Services Office on Women's Health reports that the number of people in the US affected by eating disorders doubled between the 1970s and 1990s.
- In the 1970s, 6 per cent of teenagers worried about their weight: it's now up to 40 per cent.
- Twenty years ago models weighed 20 per cent less than the average woman – that's one fifth of your entire body weight; and today's models have pared it down to 23 per cent.

Average woman

Ms Average is 5'4", weighs 145 lb. and wears a size 12–14 dress, a 36C bra and size 6 shoes. Compare this to a popular fashion doll who is 6'0", weighs 101 lb., wears a size 6 dress, has a 39" bust, a 19" waist, and a hip size of 33". Or a shop mannequin: normally 6'0", dress size 8, has a 34" bust, 23" waist and 34" hips. No wonder most of us get depressed when we're shopping!

Maybe you've heard the expression 'There are over three billion women in the world who do not look like supermodels, and only eight who do.'

One of the ironies is that many don't realise or remind themselves that the model on the magazine cover or in the ad doesn't really exist. 'She' is airbrushed. If you met the model in person you probably wouldn't recognise her because she doesn't actually look like that! For decades, we've learned to overlook the fact that a skilled, professional commercial artist is paid to take a photo of a model and use an airbrush to change the length of her legs, take away every blemish on her face, smooth where her skin should fold, add colour or whiteness to her eyes and teeth, add a crevice-like shadow to her cleavage, and put that on the front of a popular women's magazine.

Women look at that and think, 'Wow! But I don't look like that . . . If I bought that beauty cream then I would look more like her . . . If I went on that diet I would look more like that . . . ' But the woman in the photo doesn't even exist. And it's even easier now with computers. It is amazing what you can do with computer graphics!

Am I just being hysterical?

Fair question! But did you know that just a few minutes of looking at models in a fashion magazine can cause many women to feel depressed, guilty and shameful?

These images really do affect us. We see these fictional images and think, 'Right, another diet . . . ' There are so many crazy diets out there – I've even seen a chocolate diet. (No, I *won't* tell you where to find it!) We'll try them all to lose any weight we can so that we can look more the way we want to look – or at least to reward ourselves with a new outfit.

Maybe it's not so different for boys

As women, it doesn't help us with our self-esteem when we are constantly confronted with pictures of beautiful models with tiny waists and porcelain teeth, but it isn't just women who have standards to live up to. It isn't as relentless for men, but they're faced with biceps of steel and stomach muscle six-packs too. We need to remember that men struggle with eating disorders.

It seems to be more socially acceptable, even admirable, for a man to be compulsive about exercise or sports

Whether skinny or chubby, many young boys in school are faced with physical intimidation and bullying. I recently read in a magazine that bodybuilding was the answer to how to be safe from bullies and admired by girls. You only need to look at the whole bodybuilding industry with all of the clubs, machines, high-priced nutritional supplements and even drugs to see how popular it has become. And what's it all for? To attain a perfect body image!

Also, it seems to be more socially acceptable, even admirable, for a man to be compulsive about exercise or sports.

The point being . . .

Now please understand that I'm not saying that all fashion is evil, or that it's immoral to want to look and feel good. And, as I said, I'm not saying that the media *causes* our insecurities and problems. Most of us get by just fine. But the images are so pervasive that it's like a steady tide or current pushing everyone in its direction. It shapes our thinking, our tastes, our standards and our hopes the way those dramatic-looking trees growing on a wind-swept shoreline are shaped – the tree is still growing up, but you can see how it's shaped by the *constant* push of the wind. And for those of us who have weaknesses and insecurities, especially while growing up – we may not have the inner strength to spring back.

Set up for futility

So, now we're looking at a combination of two dynamics which can set someone up for an eating disorder: inwardly weakened and dissatisfied people facing external cultural pressures to achieve the impossible – day in and day out. Perhaps the worst part is that most don't recognise the futility, so it just becomes this nagging dissatisfaction, frustration or depression. 'It should be better. There's got to be a way for me to turn out better.' It can be tough for a young woman to keep things in perspective as she matures.

So (getting back to my own story) with all this going on around me, here I am about to enter my teen years.

3

Beginning

This is how it started for me – how I went from having insecurities about myself to being trapped in a fully-fledged eating disorder.

As I explained before, I started with a really bad image of myself – I had a lot of teasing in school.

Off to a bad start

The self-image thing didn't get any better when the family moved and I arrived at a new school. And you know how quickly someone new gets sized up – basically, by how they look. Well my next-older sister, Michelle, was accepted at once as she was pretty, wore lots of make-up, short tight skirts and high heels. I opted for a long skirt and comfortable shoes – sensible, but a big mistake socially.

I learned that image = acceptance

Granted, I was only twelve and wasn't yet interested in fashion, but from watching my older sisters (especially the one in my school) I learned that appearance was your ticket to being noticed and liked, and having friends. From then on I felt I was playing catch-up and my appearance just wasn't helping. On the one hand, my mum would reassure me, 'You're beautiful, Maxine.' But on the other hand, I was being called ugly and teased at school.

So I learned that *image = acceptance.*

Sister, sister

A couple of years later Michelle was my first exposure to an eating disorder: in her case anorexia.

Michelle went off to college to study Art and Design. She was particularly interested in textile design, so she was surrounded by the kind of fashion images we've been talking about. She had never been fat, but each time she came home from college to visit she was thinner . . . and thinner . . . and thinner. We didn't know this, but at college she went all day without eating anything except one apple at lunch and then tried to go all evening without eating anything else. If she did have a 'proper' lunch, she would 'make up for it' by going to the pool to exercise. So she was pushing herself physically as well. Today we would call her pattern anorexic, but back then we'd just call it 'being on a diet and exercising.'

There wasn't much talk about eating disorders in the 1980s, but what was happening with my sister's weight was a bit of a mystery and my parents were beginning to wonder.

Now ours was one of those families with a lot of emotional insecurity and tension, so we weren't really able to discuss things heart-to-heart. Therefore the root issues that were pulling Michelle down weren't likely to be addressed in any helpful way. So one evening my dad just did what he felt he could in the circumstances. He told her, 'If you don't start eating, we are not going to pay for

your college tuition.' And that was that. He essentially
forced her to begin eating by threatening her dream of
having a career in Art and Design. And to a degree it
worked. For years she continued to struggle, but when
she came home she *looked* like she was taking better care
of herself. The outward symptoms at least were beaten.

Who's watching now?

In the meantime, there I was in the background, watching
all this. And during all the drama I, the younger sister,
noticed that Michelle was the centre of an awful lot of
attention. Although it was in the form of a 'Now hear this
. . . ' ultimatum, I saw Dad show that he cared. So here I
was, approaching my teenage years still insecure about
myself and needing support and encouragement, particularly from my own father, and I saw him express love
the only way he could. It made me jealous.

And you know, my sister got a *lot* of compliments
through it all. She has always been pretty, but then people
started commenting specifically about how 'nice and
thin' she had become. Of course I noticed too – I wasn't
getting such compliments. Not from anyone.

I'm three years younger than Michelle and I naturally
admired and looked up to *My-big-sister-studying-Art-and-
Design-in-college*. I looked at myself and thought, 'Hmm,
I'm younger than her and yet I'm fatter . . . I should lose
some weight too.'

Getting in on the act

So it seemed like it would be a good idea if I tried going
on a diet. But there were obstacles: I loved food, I hated
feeling hungry and I hated exercising. So when I tried to

diet, I always got too hungry and quickly gave it up and just ate what I wanted anyway. Having failed, my conclusion was, 'Ah, forget this. . . . I can't do it. . . . What's the point?'

So it wasn't working. But you can see that I'd already come to some conclusions:

- I hated myself and wanted to change.
- Looking better (thinner) would help me have friends and fit in.
- I was failing at doing anything about it.
- If I could get past the discomfort, I could be noticed and complimented.
- If it went wrong, it might at least mean that my dad would notice me and show me love.

Nibble overload

When I was eighteen, I moved from England to Sweden to work in an institutional kitchen. Suddenly, I was surrounded by food all the time, handling it, smelling it, serving it and so on. My mum is Swedish, and we had visited a number of times, but my Swedish wasn't very good – one of the cooks asked for a platter, a *carotta*, and I brought her a bunch of carrots! Well, what would you do?

So it was hard to connect socially and I was getting a bit lonely. The job also made it all too easy to nibble food throughout the day. 'Just a little one of these. . . . I'll get rid of this broken one. . . . Oh, these are my favourites. . . . '

So, before long, I put on quite a bit of weight – 30lb. Looking back on it, I can see I was just eating something 'nice' as a way of filling the void in my heart because deep down I was unhappy. But also I was starting

> *'I will never be fat again.' This kind of vow, sometimes called an inner vow, can have lasting impact*

unhealthy habits of eating continuously throughout the day with absolutely no self-discipline. I had no idea how long it would take to unlearn these habits.

In the summer, I went to the coast to visit family. I remember sitting on the beach in my bikini feeling very self-conscious. My auntie, who hadn't seen me for a while, was there too. She took one look at me, and with raised eyebrows she started to laugh, and said, 'Maxine, what has *happened* to you?'

I remember the feeling vividly. It was like a sword running through my heart. Not just because of what she said and how she said it, but it shocked me because I was in denial of the fact that I had become fat. And in that startled, vulnerable moment my reflex was to make a vow in my heart: 'I will *never* be fat again.' (This kind of vow, sometimes called an inner vow, can have lasting impact. It's like an old landmine or depth charge waiting to go off, or buried toxins leaking into the ground. Everybody needs to make decisions in life, but these decisions can be charged with a negative emotion i.e. embarrassment, anger, fear etc. If this happens, these destructive patterns can become part of the way you think, even take on a life of their own. Even after the momentary pain subsides, it's like a deep part of us keeps trying to fulfil the command.)

To make matters worse, Maria, my older sister, was pregnant with her first child, which led to jokes about why I was bigger than her. And when Michelle wanted to borrow some of my clothes, she found them far too big. So it was a summer of joking and teasing. Of course, I joked along on the outside. But on the inside I was hurting and hated myself even more.

Objectively you could say it shouldn't have been a big deal, but I felt so ridiculed and rejected for the way I looked. Not only did it wound me, but I hated myself for being fat. I was really frustrated because I just couldn't diet. I'd tried every possible way I knew, so I felt trapped and ashamed.

And then I read something new in a magazine . . .

Get rid of it?

I read an article about this girl who would eat whatever she liked . . . and then she would make herself sick to get rid of it. The article jumped off the page at me, and I thought, 'What a brilliant idea! Now I can have my cake, eat it . . . and then just get rid of it. Nobody needs to know. And I can be thin.'

At this point, I didn't even know bulimia existed, otherwise I might have known it was dangerous. (I don't even remember if the article said that what the girl was doing was a problem.) It sounds a bit crazy now, but to me it was something that looked like it might work.

Now if you don't struggle with this specific pattern, then I understand if it doesn't make sense to you. But so many people tell me about how they reached the point where they were fed up with continually failing at diets and said they had thought about making themselves sick but just couldn't do it. I wish it had been too horrible for me, because it becomes a terrible cycle that is very hard to break.

4

Body Behaviour

*B*efore moving on, I need to interrupt my story and back up to an earlier point I made about food being a comfort.

By now, you may be asking, 'What is it about eating?' Maybe you know that feeling when you've had a rough day at work or school and you get home and you go straight to the refrigerator: 'It's been a bad day. I just want something nice.' Why don't we have a nap instead, go for a walk, watch TV . . . maybe you do those things? Some of us turn to food. Especially snacks.

And for most people this is just normal and mostly harmless. But for others, there's a link to something way below the surface. I believe God has shown me that eating for comfort opens the way to a deeper need in people who struggle with their eating patterns.

First food = first comfort

The very first discomfort that we go through in life, the first trauma (assuming a normal pregnancy) is – to be born. Can you imagine what it's like for a baby to actually go through that? That's a physically and emotionally over-whelming up-and-down experience for such a little thing. No wonder babies cry!

I believe that the depth of the emotional link with food spills over into the spiritual dimension of our lives

I won't expand on all that the baby goes through, but think about this. At the end of all that confusion and pain, what's the first comfort and relief we get? It's our mother's breast – suddenly there's this new pleasure of our first food, and oh, it feels good and we're being held so warm and close, and we're feeling so much better . . .

This is how and where a baby bonds with her mother. I believe this is also where we forge the connection between relief from anxiety and pain with comfort, security and food. It goes that far back. (I believe too that the depth of the emotional link with food spills over into the spiritual dimension of our lives.)

So am I saying this is all just psychological? Partly, but it's also a physical, medical fact, having to do with how food affects our body chemistry.

Why certain foods appeal

Have you wondered why we'll so often turn to a particular *type* of food, especially something sweet? For some people, it might be something starchy, like popcorn or bread. Maybe you're one of the sensible ones who reach for the celery sticks, but for most people, sugars and starches hold an appeal all their own.

Food as a drug

This might surprise you, but sugar is actually a depressant. Yes, there is an initial rush of energy, which would make you think it's a stimulant, but the effect quickly dissipates and leaves the nervous system depressed and produces a numb feeling. Unless we continue to feed more sugar into our system to fuel that surge of energy, we crash. The result is like that of a mild depressant drug.

Now what happens if you take sugar away? Have you ever tried to cut sugar out of your diet? Have you noticed how irritable you get? You might get a headache, feel angry and restless. That's a chemical withdrawal. A lot of people experience the same symptoms when they stop taking caffeine. And the connection with starchy snacks, like crisps, is that the carbohydrates are actually complicated forms of sugar, which break down into simpler sugars in your system. The sugars have the same effect as I've already mentioned, but it's buffered somewhat by the intermediate step of digestion, so the take-off and landing are smoother!

Addictive food

Now to get a bit more technical just for a minute, there are two types of brain chemicals involved in food addiction: serotonin and endorphin. Both of these chemicals make us feel good, more relaxed, give us relief from pain and decrease stress.

Serotonins and endorphins are released when we digest sugars, whether it's simple sugar, like we have in sweets or in our tea, or complex sugars in the form of carbohydrates. And they show up pretty consistently in normal diets as sauces, pasta, potatoes, white bread, cereal products, snacks and other baked goods. (If you want a surprise, take a look at where sugar is in the order of ingredients in your favourite brand of ketchup.)

For a lot of people that's almost their entire diet right there, so you can see how available and innocent and normal the addictive aspect of food can seem – and how that steady supply of pleasurable food-based chemicals released into the bloodstream could be addictive for them. (The women-and-chocolate theme is a popular subject these days. There is a reason that women appreciate chocolate, and it isn't just marketing hype. There's an active ingredient in chocolate called theobromine [literally 'food of the gods'] and its chemical effect is very similar to the changes in body chemistry we experience when we're in love. This explains a lot of the success of chocolate St Valentine's Day gifts!)

So although there are emotional (and spiritual) aspects to food problems, it's important to understand that in the background there are physiological influences at work too. Body chemistry and its effects on our moods and behaviour is an important factor that can exaggerate, or diminish, our personal struggles

So although there are emotional (and spiritual) aspects to food problems, it's important to understand that in the background there are physiological influences at work too. Body chemistry and its effects on our moods and behaviour is an important factor that can exaggerate, or diminish, our personal struggles.

We learn by experience (maybe without thinking it all the way through) that certain foods really do relax us, numb us, and soothe our discomfort – it's a painkiller. So when you've had a bad day and you are feeling 'Augggh!' and you reach for a chocolate bar, it's because you expect it to actually do something for you.

It's the same if you go for a jog because that releases endorphins and it makes you feel good: you get a runner's high. According to a nutritionist I spoke to, the same thing happens with a really spicy curry. (Another interesting phenomenon: in England, the best East Indian restaurants are often in the nightclub districts. My theory for this business trend is that after the dance clubs empty out you can see the curry houses fill up with aerobicised clubbers already riding on a wave of endorphins from dancing, alcohol and who-knows-what-else. What better chemical stimulus to top it all off than a piping dansak or balti? We need to understand that when it comes to food, there's more involved than our taste buds or an empty stomach!)

What I'm saying, in other words, is . . . it's not 'all in your head.' And if you struggle with guilt in this area, it may help to know that what you've been up against is more complicated than simple whims and mild notions.

5

Battle in the Mind

*N*ow in the beginning phase of my bulimia, it wasn't all that scary because it was like, 'OK, you had ice cream, you've broken your diet, so just get rid of it and start again.' But it didn't take long before it started to take control of my mind and the first thing I would think of when I woke up in the morning was, 'OK. *Today* I am going to lose weight; I am not going to eat badly . . . *Today* I am going to work on my goal to be thin . . . I'm not going to eat *today* . . . '

Well, I'd get halfway through the day and I'd get so hungry and run to the fridge just to find something to eat, but once I started, I could not stop! 'Just *one* more spoonful of ice cream then I'll stop. . . . Just a little slice of cake . . . and a bit more . . . oops, all gone!' Once I started I could not stop and, before I knew it, the whole ice cream carton was empty and the cake was gone, as well as half of Mum's homemade biscuits. Then came the guilt and shame.

My guilty thoughts started to have voices of their own. 'Look at you! You're so fat and ugly! You're useless! You can't even keep to a simple diet! Now you're going to get really fat.' And I'd run to the bathroom to get rid of everything in me.

Then came the calm after the storm. Relief again. I could feel my mind and body settling down. But not without feeling ashamed as once more I had broken my promise to God that I'd never do it again.

And so it went on: every day the same.

Food invades the mind

Do you relate to this? For the short time you're eating that chocolate bar, it feels good: you stop thinking about what is going on outside; your mind is not focused on how you feel about yourself; you forget about what just happened, the things that get you down; and for those few moments there is a bit of satisfaction.

The problem is it doesn't last very long. As soon as you have eaten the chocolate bar the guilt starts, the shame starts. 'Why did I do it? Why did I eat that? I hate myself. I feel awful . . . ' It's just this horrible, horrible cycle.

Destructive cycle

For the person who is trapped in this kind of cycle, the feeling that they are alone in it and won't be understood by others is a big part of why the problem seems so over-whelming.

And so this cycle started for me. I was desperate for comfort so I would eat but I hated feeling full and fat and would get rid of it all. At first I was in control but before long it controlled me. It started with getting rid of just junk food but, before long, as soon as I had eaten even a normal meal I simply could not keep it inside me. I had started something and I couldn't turn it off. It was out of control.

For an anorexic person, it's different

In the case of an anorexic person, the pattern is both similar and different. The similarity is that it begins with dieting so that you can be happier with yourself. The difference is that, rather than a lack of willpower and control, the anorexic's willpower takes over completely.

It's like a destructive self-discipline. You might say it's similar to that feeling that you get when you've made it through a fast or had some hard exercise – it kind of hurts, but it feels like you've done yourself some good. An anorexic can feel like they're accomplishing something by exercising their will and restraining themselves from eating.

The hook is that someone who is anorexic is already experiencing some other emotional or mental pain (like dissatisfaction with themselves or depression, loneliness, insecurity or resentment) and it's usually something that is beyond their control – something that is happening *to them*, or to their life. So the sense of 'accomplishment' from self-denial and withholding food from themselves (almost always with the goal of looking better by losing weight) makes them feel as if they are finally winning . . . in one area, at least.

The actual root of their problems aren't touched by losing weight – they are still unhappy, especially with themselves and how they look

What they can't see for themselves is that they are addicted to that false sense of accomplishment and self-denial. The actual root of their problems (rejection, sorrow etc.) aren't touched by losing weight – they are still unhappy, especially with themselves and how they look, so desperation makes them keep trying the same thing, but – trying harder. Losing weight becomes their obsession because they have found that skipping meals is something they can 'succeed' at – 'I haven't eaten all day.' So they focus on this little victory of not eating because they feel so defeated everywhere else.

It's like obsessively polishing the same glass over and over because you can't face cleaning the oven – the kitchen isn't getting any cleaner, but that glass is looking better!

So the cycle looks like this: an anorexic woman is unhappy so she decides to lose weight (she's already linked the two); she loses weight, but it isn't enough because she's still unhappy; so she tries harder with a more severe diet. In time, she becomes so focused on her goal of losing weight that she can't see that it has become an obsession; and her obsession makes her think she's still not thin enough because she's still unhappy. In fact she can't even see that she's already too thin.

I knew things were out of my control when I was crossing my own moral boundaries, which is a sign of addiction

By this point, her self-discipline has become self-destructive and is shutting down her own body. And her obsession with losing weight keeps her own mind from recognising that she's too thin. She can actually look at a picture of another anorexic woman and see that the woman is too thin, and then look at herself in the mirror and still think that she should lose weight.

Betraying your own boundaries

It takes a lot of energy and work to keep this kind of obsession going. In my own case, I knew it was out of control when I was crossing my own moral boundaries, which is a sign of addiction.

Let me explain. In order for me to keep getting away with what I was doing with food, I had to lie, and be very good at lying. Food was disappearing, vast amounts of food, and I was disappearing to the bathroom every time I ate – including slipping away from the table at meal times.

The games begin

Now getting back to my story: I was back living at home, and I would do anything to avoid suspicion, to keep what I was doing a secret. Doing this covertly in my own home meant I had to be sneaking past my own family.

It sounds ridiculous, but when these patterns take hold, they consume you. I would go babysitting and as soon as the mum and dad had gone, it would be, 'Great!' – straight to the fridge – 'What have they got?' And there would always be a wide range of goodies to nibble at. I would very carefully cut little pieces off the cake and cheeses so the parents couldn't tell what I'd done. That was bad enough, but then the compulsion kicked in to keep eating until I was full. I could not stop myself. I didn't care if the kids were screaming or throwing things or whatever, I was in the kitchen on a mission! And I would not stop until I felt ill. I was that desperate to fill myself.

Today I can look back and even laugh at some of it, but at the time the deception was awful. Sometimes these kids would have an entire cupboard full of sweets of their own. I would eat far too many and then the parents would come home and I would say, 'Oh, the kids were terrible tonight. I had to give them loads of sweets to keep them quiet.' When it was me – I had eaten them!

The secret becomes your life

I know it sounds terrible, and believe me it's embarrassing to talk about now, but I had to lie like this to keep it
all secret. I was eighteen years old; it wasn't as if I was a
little kid. But I had this fear: 'If anybody knew what I am
doing . . .'

You get good at the deception. And the more you lie
the more separated you become from people and reality.
It's like you live this secret double life . . . a separate exis-
tence.

When food disappeared at home I'd blame my little
sister. I'd steal ice cream from the kitchen where I worked.
At the local supermarket I helped myself to the pick-and-
mix snacks and ate while shopping. I'd occasionally get
caught helping myself to a third piece of cake at parties. I
even tucked food up my sleeves for later . . . the list goes
on.

My eyes started to become bloodshot most of the time
because of the physical strain of throwing up. I kept my
fingernails short so I wouldn't scratch the back of my
throat. My voice was hoarse and my throat was sore so I
chewed gum. Some girls even teach themselves to vomit
at will.

The burden of guilt

Now on the inside we know when we are violating our
own moral boundaries – we don't want anybody to even
look at us, especially when we're eating. Why is that?
Why aren't you free to eat in front of people? But it's as if
you *can't*, you just want to hide away, or take the packet
of biscuits to your room so nobody can see. There is a
shame; there is guilt.

There was no way I could go to the church or to God with this, although I'd been a Christian since I was very young. And yet I wasn't denying God, I just couldn't come to him with my struggle. After every time I made myself sick, it was like I'd stand far off at a distance and tell him: 'I promise I won't make myself sick again. I promise I won't do it.' But every day I would fail. And each time I did it, I just felt guiltier, more condemned, more useless, more of a failure.

Any secret sin that you are practising can take a hold and Satan uses that as an opportunity to get in there and mix his accusations in with your own guilty thoughts

Secrecy

One of the dynamics here is that when you walk in any sin, especially secretly, it takes a hold of your mind. It doesn't have to be about food – any secret sin that you are practising can take a hold and Satan uses that as an opportunity to get in there and mix his accusations in with your own guilty thoughts.

While I was going through this period, I would always hear those same voices, 'You're fat! You're ugly! You're no good! You can't even stick to a simple diet! Do you think God loves you? You can't even do this! Not only that, you lie about it continuously, all the time, every day . . . '

Keep on keepin' on

At the same time, while all of this was going on inside, I was trying to keep up a strong front and, incredibly, still

On the inside, I was crying, 'I'm not as strong as everyone thinks!' I was desperate to be looked after, to be loved and cared for

thinking, 'I can do it. I'm not going to tell anybody because if I can get thin, people will like me. Then I can fit in somewhere.' You see, I was still clinging desperately to my goal of being loved. I was still trying to cope with the normal world of work, bills, chores and the occasional chance to get out and do something sociable.

I was also trying to care for others. My parents' marriage had broken up and my mum was not coping well with it. My younger sister was still just a little girl, so she had to be looked after. I was hurting too but I was pushing all of my pain into the background, keeping it shut away behind this door of secrecy, while I continued to try to get on with life and be strong for my family. I just kept going, doing what I had to. But on the inside, I was crying, 'I'm not as strong as everyone thinks!' I was desperate to be looked after, to be loved and cared for. I wanted someone to notice that I was in pain too.

This pattern was consuming everything. Everything from the time I woke up: I couldn't think of anything else except being hungry and trying not to do it again. But I did: three, four, five times a day. By the end, I was making myself sick six times a day. If you've thrown up once you know how horrible it is, but for me it was continual, every day without exception. I hated it. But it felt like I had no choice but to slip away and close the bathroom door behind me. I had tricks so nobody could hear and I'd get rid of everything within me that was making me feel full and horrible. When I threw up it would be in such a violent way it was as if I wanted to get rid of everything in me. Not just the food – everything and anything about me. I preferred the feeling of being empty. I wanted to starve myself; I didn't want to feed

That was the loneliest, most desperate time for me: in the bathroom

my body. So if I could only get rid of it all . . . . I just wanted to punish myself, hurt myself in some way.

That was the loneliest, most desperate time for me: in the bathroom. I can remember that so clearly. I desperately wanted to cry out for help but I couldn't. I didn't know what to say. I was just so immersed in my own pain that I couldn't believe there was a way out.

So I was living a double life. If you had met me, I would have seemed to be fine, coping well with my parents' split and being a support to my family. What you wouldn't see was that my whole world was crumbling on the inside and nobody seemed to realise. This was my secret and I had to keep it. I was too ashamed to tell anyone.

An eating disorder is really a silent cry for love, care and acceptance, or at least help. As someone who has cried out silently many times, I'm now trying to put words to those cries for help, which maybe you can't yet do.

Attention starved

A big part of my eating disorder was looking for attention that I never received as a child. I'd already seen that Michelle got attention for being thin, so I knew it worked. I didn't just want attention from friends and boys – I wanted it from my parents. I wanted them to be worried about me, to show some kind of concern.

An eating disorder is really a silent cry for love, care and acceptance, or at least help

Even bad attention (like being angry with me) was, at least, attention. But they always seemed so busy. There was always someone else to worry about.

I remember that as a young child I used to take a nail clipper or scissors and scratch my face with them and then say I'd hurt myself or that my baby sister had scratched me. I enjoyed the attention it gave me. I used to wish I could break my arm and get a cast like my brother had, just so I would be noticed too. Looking back on it all, I now see that what I'd done at the childish level I was doing in an adult way through my bulimia.

Turning away from life

Deep down, I just wanted to be little again. I didn't want to grow up. Even more, I began to wish desperately that I'd never been born. I hated life and often wondered how I could kill myself. But being a Christian I always believed that if you killed yourself you'd go to hell. So there didn't seem to be much choice.

However, after days, weeks, months, even a couple of years of this, I eventually felt I was shutting down. After a while, there were no good or bad days. I started to feel less and less as I went on using food. I was detaching . . . going numb.

Even turning towards death

That detachment led to a resignation to the idea of dying as a way out. I just wanted some way to escape the pain.

I wanted it to be over. Basically, I *wanted* to die. I developed a death wish. Many anorexic and bulimic women do.

I started to fantasise, rehearsing the scenes surrounding my death. How would I be discovered? What would people say? Who would be shocked? Would anyone care – even notice?

I've noticed when praying for anorexic women that it can be difficult because although they're asking for help with their eating problem, at the same time they're also desperate just to be cared for and loved, and to be healed would mean an end to the care and attention they're finally getting. A woman can find she's finally getting the prayer, sympathy, understanding and love she has missed.

In fact, you may find that although an anorexic woman wants the food problem to go away, she doesn't want the care to stop. In a sense, she's having to face growing up and caring for herself. Often, she'll prefer to let things carry on and have to go to hospital again and again to receive care. Some die in order to get that care. An anorexic may not be ready to let go of their problem (which is really a problem of their will) because they still have this mission in their heart to be loved – they have to be thin enough to be loved; that desire for love still hasn't been satisfied and they would rather die trying to get that love.

I have spoken to so many parents who are desperate and feel helpless – they just don't know what to do. One mother told me, 'We have tried everything from forcing her to eat to ignoring her in the hope she'd get over this but it is getting worse.'

Parents, if you have an anorexic child, the most important thing you can do is to just love them. And express it by spending time with them, doing things for them,

A love deficit is love we should have received as a child: when we don't, it leaves a deficit, a hole

telling them you love them, nurturing them, encouraging them, complimenting them, hugging them, giving them lots of attention – even if it seems immature and not very grown up. An anorexic girl needs to catch up on a love deficit. A love deficit is love we should have received as a child: when we don't, it leaves a deficit, a hole. Forget about food for a while and concentrate on loving her. Once she feels loved, she will want to live and will want to eat again. Taking the harsh approach of 'Pull yourself together!' just isn't going to work.

6

Breaking Out

The turning point for me came one day when I made myself sick and I coughed up blood. It shocked and scared me. I remember crying myself to sleep that night, saying, 'God, you have to help me. I don't want to live any more. I hate my life. I can't keep on doing this to myself.'

Then I felt the Lord say, 'You need to tell your mum.'

'Oh Lord, I don't want to tell her. She won't understand – what am I going to say? I feel so ashamed and embarrassed.'

This is something Satan will always throw at you when you are about to bring something into the light that has been hidden. 'You can't tell anyone! They won't understand!' 'You will look like a freak!' 'Keep it hidden; it's better that way.' Satan knows that as long as something stays hidden he has control over you.

Bringing it into the light with a parent

But the Lord gave me the right moment. I told my mum one night.

'There's something I haven't told you: I make myself sick. I've been doing it for years and I can't stop.' She was shocked and we cried together.

My mother's first reaction was guilt and shame. She felt she had failed as a parent not to have noticed what I was going through. This made me feel worse than I already did, as I now felt guilty for telling my mum.

(If you are a parent of someone suffering with an eating disorder it can be difficult to come to terms with your child's suffering. I advise that you don't take on guilt and shame but focus on your child at this point and give all the love and encouragement you can.)

Telling my mum was an important step, I wasn't alone in this any more and, for the first time in a very long while, I was able to admit: I NEED HELP!

But unfortunately, it didn't end there. Mum prayed for me and I told her I'd stop making myself sick, but the problem was I couldn't, which meant that now I knew my mum was watching me I had to be even more secretive!

Bringing it into the light spiritually

I began to realise that there was a spiritual element to my struggle – that it wasn't just physical and mental. The voices I'd been hearing in my head were getting stronger: 'You're fat, ugly and stupid . . . You're an absolute idiot . . . You're useless! You can't stop! You'll never be free.' And so the voices continued.

When you are in some kind of sin and you've been in it for a long time, something happens when you bring it out into the light. The enemy starts to lose his grip

I was getting even more desperate and I knew I had to bring my problem to the church. It wasn't normal to hear about this kind of thing at church, but by now

I was so desperate that I just thought, 'I don't care what anybody thinks, I'm asking for help! I *need* help.'

We went to an evening meeting, and towards the end of the service someone asked if anyone needed prayer. I practically ran to the front of the congregation and told everyone what I'd been doing and that I needed help. The church was quite stunned by such honesty and vulnerability, but people gathered around and prayed for me.

And *that* broke it

You must understand this: when you are in some kind of sin and you've been in it for a long time, something happens when you bring it out into the light. The enemy (Satan) starts to lose his grip.

Telling someone was the first stage of my recovery. And it was important that I told people who had authority in my life: in this case my mum and my church. Precisely the people I'd wanted to keep it all from.

If you have an eating disorder, then it is *crucial* that you break any secrecy. Bring it out into the light! Tell someone what you're doing, what you're struggling with, what it's like, what you're doing to hide it. And tell someone who is in spiritual authority over you – your parents, your spouse, your pastor. If you just tell a friend, it's too easy to get around them, put them off, stop listening to them. It should be someone who can speak into your life, encourage you in a meaningful way, and someone you'd allow to correct you.

There's another powerful dynamic in your making this decision to bring your struggle into the light: it's a point of turning, a change in direction, part of letting go of your ability to exert your own control (or lack of it) over yourself. The way to get past this is to humble yourself and reach out to those in higher authority – see Proverbs 28:13. It was at this point that God set me free from bulimia. It was broken. And I never made my self sick again.

A new beginning is only the start

When I got prayer at church, the battle, the fighting, stopped, and my victory had been won. However, the post-war process of re-building had just begun.

At the time, it was such a relief that I thought, 'That's it! I have confessed it. I don't make myself sick any more and I'm OK. I'm healed. I'm well.'

A lot of us are like that. We've confessed and been forgiven, the Lord breaks through, and we think it's over. But although for me it was a new beginning – it wasn't completely over. The Lord was saying to me, 'Maxine, no. You have missed something here. There were reasons why you were doing all that. We need to look deeper. I need to go deeper in your heart. There are huge issues here we need to look at together.'

But I was not aware of them at all. You see, I've given you a lot of information about my background and some of the weaknesses that had led up to my bulimia, but back then I hadn't connected any of those things with my problem. I'd just been getting through the hours and days trying to cope and survive. But if all it took was a couple of hurts and bad decisions to tip me into that terrible course, what would prevent me from falling back into it again when something else happened?

If I wasn't strengthened and re-built from the
inside to cope with life,
how would it go with me later?

The first practical step for me was physical healing because my stomach at that point was in such a mess that I couldn't eat anything. So I went to a doctor, but I can remember I was too ashamed to say what I had been doing. I just said I had stomach troubles, so they did all these different tests, and I started a life of special diets. At one point, all I could eat was boiled carrots, potatoes and yoghurt. This wasn't too exciting . . . all the foods I'd been using as my comfort and joy were gone! The feeling of emptiness was incredible. But eventually I was well enough to get back to a fairly normal life. I just needed to eat sensibly.

> *The Lord is continuing to walk me through the process of sorting through the root causes and the consequences in my life. It hadn't been simple, and not always easy, but the freedom is worth it!*

When the healing begins

I'm differentiating here between a disorder being broken, and being healed. There are wonderful stories of people being miraculously and instantaneously healed from such things. Those stories are great, and I hope that will be your experience, but you may be looking at a healing *process*. And that will take some time, more insight and plenty of understanding. It's been like that for me, and the Lord is continuing to walk me through the process of sorting through the root causes and the consequences in my life. It hasn't been simple, and not always easy, but the freedom is worth it!

Three years later, the Lord opened a door for me to go to Canada for the School of Ministry at the Toronto Airport Christian Fellowship. I had always wanted to go to a ministry school to learn more about God and when I heard about this school I knew it was the right thing for me to do. It was here that I went through a lot of emotional healing, the healing of my heart. But, to be honest, I had no idea I needed it. On the outside I had it fairly together: I was twenty-three and seemed to have a real zeal for life and adventure.

But the Lord said to me, 'It is time to look at the real pain. Are you going to let me take you back there? Take you back to some of those really painful times that you have been pushing down? That you haven't wanted to look at? That you have been avoiding as you let life go on?'

I thought I'd come to the School of Ministry because I was going to be equipped and filled with revival fire to get out there and help save the nations . . . But behind the zeal and enthusiasm was this girl who was still very hurt and in need of healing, desperately wanting to be small, to not have to grow up and take on responsibilities. I didn't see it coming, but the Lord was about to take me back to my family again!

7

Back to the Roots

To really be free, there's more involved than stopping the behaviour, whether it's bingeing, or purging, or withholding food from yourself. You can expect that there will also be a process of settling those deep issues which made you vulnerable to falling into eating problems and then held you there.

The healing begins

I'm now going to share with you some examples of the work the Lord has been doing to heal my heart from the things that hardened it over the years and made me vulnerable to an eating disorder. Your own history will obviously be different, but my story should help as an example of the kinds of things you'll need to work through with the Lord's help and guidance.

Getting real with 'Dad'

While I was in Toronto, Canada, for the School of Ministry, one of the key teachings was about God being restored to us as our Father. Peter Jackson, then the School's Director, was speaking about God loving us as a father loves a child. Peter shared his testimony about how he had met God as his Father only a few years ago even though he had been a Christian for years – and that meeting his Father had changed his life.

As Peter spoke his face glowed with the Father's love, and I remember thinking, 'I don't know the God he knows.' I was scared of thinking of God as a father because my own experience of a dad had been difficult but I also knew that I desperately wanted what Peter had. I listened night after night to people telling their stories at the front of the church. People shared about how they had met God as a father.

I remember one man's story as it really stuck in my mind. He had been a pastor of a church for years and had been faithfully serving God but had reached the end of himself. He was tired, burnt out and had decided to leave the ministry. He heard about this church in Toronto and decided as a last resort to come and visit. The night before I had noticed him because he had been rolling on the floor and laughing hysterically. He told us that God had told him that he loved him and had been tickling him, which was why he had been rolling around on the floor! And as he shared his experience, tears were rolling down his face. He said, 'Even though I have been a Christian for years, pastored a church, I never knew my Father. But yesterday I heard him tell me that he loves me and that I am his son!' (I wish I knew the name of this man to be able to give you his name, but I don't!)

As he spoke those words I knew this was what I wanted! This was what I had been waiting to hear all my life: that God loved me and that I was his daughter.

But as I listened I felt very sad. Instead of being happy for the man, I was angry. I'd prayed and been prayed for so many times, and I hadn't experienced God's love. I hadn't had God tickle me. He'd never told me that he loved me. That night I left the meeting upset and angry. I found a quiet place away from all the people and began pouring out my heart to the Lord. 'Right, Lord, I have had enough. I can clearly see that you love all these people more than me! Why won't you meet with me in that way? Why haven't you told me that you love me?'

Before long I wasn't talking to God any more but shouting at him. I told him I hated him and that I didn't want to follow him any more. That he was a cruel father, not a loving one. By the time I had finished I had tears running down my face (and no tissue of course!).

Then there was a horrible silence as I waited for the lightning bolts from heaven to come and strike me down! I'd told God exactly what I thought of him without holding anything back . . . and now I felt like a naughty little girl waiting to be punished.

Then in the silence I heard a very quiet voice speak right into my heart. 'At last, Maxine, you are being real with me! Now we can begin a relationship.'

I couldn't believe what I heard! I had expected him to be angry but there was such love in his voice. I met with God that evening in a way I will never forget. He spoke to me about my childhood, about things that had happened while I was growing up: he showed me how he had always been there and that he loved me so much.

That evening was the beginning of getting to know God as my Father.

I believe that the most important step to being healed from an eating disorder is to get to know your heavenly Father the way he really is and to let him heal your heart. The biggest need in anyone's heart is to know that they are loved just the way they are and that they are his precious child and that he cares about them. In short, I have

The truth is we are all looking for love and acceptance that can only be found in our relationship with God.

learnt that the most important thing about being healed (and staying healed) is to really get to know God as your Father – as your daddy!

I was continually looking for love and acceptance in the way I looked: 'If I only get a little bit thinner then people will love me.' I was listening to the lies that the world feeds us. The world tells us that if you look better you will be loved, if you have more money you will be happy – but there are thin, attractive millionaires out there who will tell us they are still searching for love.

The truth is we are all looking for love and acceptance that can only be found in our relationship with God.

> I will be a Father to you, and you will be my sons and daughters, says the Lord Almighty. (2 Cor. 6:18)

> Because you are sons, God sent the Spirit of his Son into our hearts, the Spirit who calls out, 'Abba, Father'. So you are no longer a slave, but a son; and since you are a son, God has made you also an heir. (Gal. 4:6,7)

What the people of the world need more than anything is to know God as Father. But we have an enemy, Satan, who will do anything in his power to distort our picture of God. This enemy knows that if he destroys the picture of a father then we as God's children will never be able to relate to God as our loving heavenly Father.

In Exodus 34:6, we read that: 'The Lord, the Lord, the compassionate and gracious God, *slow to anger, abounding in love and faithfulness,* maintaining love to thousands and forgiving wickedness, rebellion and sin.' (My own emphasis.)

Our HEADS choose to believe Scripture . . . but our HEARTS go by the experiences we have had.

I know I didn't see God this way. I felt that because I had messed up and was struggling with bulimia, God wouldn't want anything to do with me. The reason why so many of us keep God at a distance is because we don't really know him.

Many of us base our idea of what a father is by the experience we have had with our own fathers.

The single greatest influence on your view of your heavenly Father is your earthly father.

This does not now give you license to blame every one of life's problems on your dad but I hope that this will help you understand the reason you cannot relate to God as a father. For, without a doubt, the way you relate to God as your heavenly Father will be affected and influenced by your experiences with your own dad.

What was your relationship like with your father when you were growing up?

Sadly, today we have a generation which is growing up with little or no relationship with a father. Therefore, they have no concept of what a loving father is.

As I mentioned before we have an enemy, Satan, who is desperately trying to distort the picture of Father God. He knows that if he destroys fatherhood then we as children will not be able to relate to God as a Father. Let's identify this enemy: the father of lies (John 8:44), the accuser (Revelation 12:10), the tempter (1 Corinthians 7:5). If he can destroy the image of the Father he will.

Even though the Bible is full of truth about our Father and his love for us, very often

our HEADS choose to believe Scripture . . .
but our HEARTS go by the experiences we have had.

For example if your father was the

Performance oriented father

If you are doing everything right then you receive affirmation and praise! But if you mess up, then you're met with disapproval or disappointment or 'the look'! ('The look' that tells you he is not happy.)

As a child we are taught to perform. If you're good, you're loved – if you're bad, you're not. If this has been your experience with your earthly father, this will be your experience with your heavenly Father: you try to pray, fast and work enough, because you will be less in the kingdom if you don't do enough.

So many of us strive to 'do', to work to please our Father and receive acceptance. Our motivation is fear: fear of rejection, fear of failure or disapproval so we keep on working.

In the three years I was out teaching and ministering to pastors and their congregations I met so many pastors who admitted to me that they felt like an employee of God rather than a son or daughter. That if only they could get a bigger church, more people saved, an outreach programme running, then God would be pleased with them. They didn't know God loved them just because of who they are and not because of what they do.

Can you honestly say that you know God loves you just the way you are? Do you really know that if you were never to do another thing for him as long as you lived, he would still love you?

Let's look at another kind of father.

The passive father

A father who wasn't personally involved in your life, he provided for you, you were never hungry and always had a roof over your head. But you never heard him say that he loved you. When I say 'father', a picture that comes to mind is the back of a newspaper, or someone staring at the football on TV. Is this the way you think of 'father' too? You have a father but he doesn't really know you?

People who have had passive fathers are often very committed Christians but they walk by faith, as many have not experienced God's love personally. They have no concept of a father who wants to take them out for the day or to sit down and have a heart-to-heart chat; a father who gets personally involved in their lives, a father who cares.

Then there's the absent father

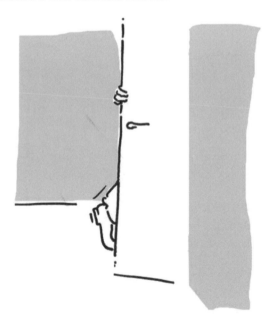

He's just not there, maybe because of death or divorce. It could be that you never knew your father. So the idea of a heavenly Father is difficult to grasp – God seems so distant and far off.

There was a man who came to me and explained that God seemed so far away and he just had no concept of him as a father. He then went on to tell me that his dad left him when he was two. He was so scared that God would reject him as well that he didn't dare come close to him.

Abusive father

Maybe your experience of a father brings back painful memories. Perhaps there was sexual, physical or emotional abuse.

If this has been your experience of a father you may have a very distorted picture of God and the thought of him being your father scares you. Unfortunately many people who have had this kind of father are nowhere near the church today and have no interest in God.

What is your picture of your heavenly Father? Does he have a frown on his face? Is he ready to hit you with his sceptre when you mess up? Or is he far away and distant?

I have nieces and nephews who love to draw pictures of their Auntie Maxine.

I usually have a huge round face, a carrot for a nose, funny looking eyes and corkscrew hair. I'm glad that their picture of me is not exactly true! I know that isn't really what I look like.

I feel like God is saying, 'You know that picture you have of me is not exactly the way I am. Will you let me show you what I am really like?'

The way you see God will even influence the way you read your Bible. I used to read Genesis and see an angry God banishing Adam and Eve from the garden, never to return. Now that I know more of my Father's character and have experienced his love, I know that he wept as they left the garden.

I remember a man coming to me after a meeting I had been speaking at. He explained that he was a pastor of a church in New Mexico. In his quiet times he felt God telling him to speak about his love. Over and over again he heard the same voice: 'Speak about my love.' He said he had been preaching on the wrath and judgement of God his whole life and didn't have one sermon on the love of God, so he decided to get on a plane and visit the church in Toronto which he had heard had a real revelation of the Father's love.

When I asked him what his experience of a dad had been he said his father had been very strict and he could now see why he saw God that way.

What was your relationship like with your father when you were growing up? Was he the kind of dad to pull you into his arms and tell you that he loved you? Did you spend time together? Did he make you feel like you were special and wanted? How is that affecting your relationship with Father God today?

My dad worked away and when he did come home was often so tired he spent a lot of his time catching up on paperwork or watching TV. My impression of God was that he was very distant and had far more important things to do than spend time with me.

Having been part of Toronto for the last seven years I have had people challenge me and say you shouldn't just go after an experience, you need to stand on the truth and what is written in God's word and that should be enough – you don't need to experience God's love.

Sadly, today we have a generation which is growing up with little or no relationship with a father. Therefore, they have no concept of what a loving father is.

Think of a newborn baby. You can tell the child that you love them, you can explain it to them verbally but that baby will not understand a word you are saying. What the baby will respond to is the soft loving tone of your voice. It is the tone that speaks of love, not the words.

A child learns how to trust through affectionate touch, through eye contact and through a loving tone of voice. The baby needs to *experience* the parents' love, not just hear about it. During World War Two, experiments were done on fifty babies. Their basic needs were taken care of but no loving physical contact was given. The babies were not held or spoken to and within six months all the babies had died. They concluded after this experiment that physical affection is essential for human survival.

We, as God's children, need to experience his love in order to really know him the way he is.

Forgiveness

No matter what your experience has been, forgiveness is the key. I challenge you to forgive your dad for misrepresenting God and ask God to come and show you what he is really like.

My father left when I was eighteen and that day I decided I didn't need a dad. But God spoke to me one day and said, 'Maxine, the day you said you didn't need a dad, you closed the door on me being your Father and I want to father you and love you back to life.'

The Lord brought back some painful memories of times I had felt so alone but he told me he would never leave me nor forsake me. I decided to open the door to being fathered by God. I was scared – what would happen? – but I knew I wanted more of this love.

The single greatest influence on your view of your heavenly Father is your earthly father.

Restoration with my own dad

As God began to restore my relationship with himself, he also began to heal my heart and bring restoration in my relationship with my own dad. After my father left our family, I was so angry I didn't ever want to see him again. My heart had grown hard towards him over the years, but as God began to love me and I chose to forgive my dad, I could feel my heart becoming softer, not only towards my own dad but towards people in general. As a result of God softening my heart, he has brought so many special friends into my life. Today I have a very good relationship with my dad and love him very much.

Anger and bitterness just act as a wall between us and the ones we love.

Healing a misshapen identity

The first step to my healing was meeting God as my Father. It was very important that I knew that God was a God of love before he began to go deeper into my heart.

God said to me, 'Now that you know me, let me take you by the hand and let me heal your heart.' God took me on a journey into my past to show me where my heart needed healing. One of the areas he began to heal was in the way I saw myself. I had hated myself and the way I looked for years but I didn't really know why.

Many people with eating disorders struggle with self-hatred. There are reasons why you dislike or even hate yourself. There are reasons why you can't love or accept yourself. And the Holy Spirit knows why.

Right back to your early schooldays, you can probably remember things that have been said that hurt or even embarrassed you. And if you can remember them, then they're still lodged in your mind somewhere – maybe they're in some remote corner, maybe they're just part of the background noise of your thoughts, humming away without bothering you too much. So should they matter? You've probably had the experience of being in a room where there's air conditioning running, or computers, or other automatic background sounds. And when those things stop and it's suddenly quiet, you feel this instant sense of relief, don't you? Yet you probably weren't thinking, 'You know, that sound is really irritating me.' In a similar way, the Lord can bring peace to the negative background noises that you listen to every day.

It is a father's job (and a mother's job) to speak life to you, to tell you that you are beautiful, to tell you that you are handsome, to tell you that you are special, that you mean something, that you are wonderful. And that instils a sense of worth, a deep trust and security in your heart.

If you have never heard those things from someone whose words you value (like a parent) you are not going to easily believe those things coming from yourself, let alone from God.

The Lord showed me during one prayer time where a root of my self-rejection had started. He just reminded me about my name. When I was born I was almost named Charlotte. I remember wondering, when I was little, why I wasn't called Charlotte. So one day I asked.

'Well, when you were born you just didn't look like a Charlotte.'

'Why? What do Charlottes look like then?'

'Well, they're kind of small and petite and pretty. And you just didn't look like that as a baby.'

As I remembered the story I began to cry, but I didn't know why. I felt a bit silly! Why was I getting so upset? It was only a story about my name.

God showed me I believed the lie that: 'I'm too big and ugly to be called Charlotte, so that's why I'm Maxine.'

There was this little lie sown into my thinking and things naturally came along to reinforce it. Even the first part of my name means 'big'. I was always teased and called 'Big Mac' and 'Maxi-pad' etc. So when the Lord reminded me of that, I thought, 'Did that really hurt me so much? Did that really go so deep?'

But the Lord said, 'There is something else that I want to show you.'

As I started to pray I heard the words in my mind, 'Your dad always wanted a boy called Gareth.'

I am the third girl in the family (there are five kids) and when I was expected my parents thought I was going to be a boy, and my name was going to be Gareth. Well, obviously I wasn't a boy! My brother, who came after me, is named Gareth. But why was God talking to me about this?

When I was growing up I hated anything to do with girls, I didn't like dresses or anything frilly. At all my birthday parties I would be the only little girl with trousers on. My mum used to plead with me to wear dresses – and grow my hair long, but I always used to make sure she cut it short like my brother Gareth's. I didn't like dolls! I used to try to be tough like the boys and play football, climb trees and beat them all at marbles. The truth was I didn't want to be a girl and I loved it when people mistook me for a boy.

The Lord was showing me another lie I had believed about myself. I believed that if I had been a boy then my dad would have really loved me. I kept hearing the words over and over again in my head: 'Your dad always wanted a boy called Gareth.' As God started to speak to me I cried. I had always felt like a huge mistake. If only I

I am a daughter.

could have been a boy then my dad would have loved me but instead I was just another girl.

Then God spoke into my heart again – he had planned me. I wasn't a mistake. He knew I was a girl and it was he who chose my name. God's words were simple but they went deep! I felt a peace come over me – it was as if I was smiling on the inside. I just kept hearing him say: 'I love you, I choose you to be my beautiful little girl.'

I had never felt special before but at that moment, when God told me he loved me, I felt special. I knew I was his and he had planned me to be a girl and had chosen my name.

Now if you asked my mum or dad if they wanted me and loved me they would have said 'Of course!' They had no idea I was feeling like one huge mistake! But even as a very small child I had come to that conclusion and even though it wasn't truth to my parents it was absolutely the truth to me.

This is how powerful lies in our lives can be. I have a friend who believed the lie that he was stupid. To this day he is still trying to prove to himself and the rest of the world that he is not stupid and he will make something of himself.

After this ministry time I noticed I began to change – not only on the inside but on the outside too. I had always hidden behind jeans and baggy T-shirts but I started wanting to look more feminine and even began to wear make-up. I felt a confidence inside that had never been there before.

People began to give me compliments. In the past I would have shrugged these off but now I found myself saying 'Thank you!' and actually receiving them. I was able to accept and enjoy being a woman for the first time in my life. I felt like the ugly duckling that had turned into a beautiful swan.

Attention from the boys

Due to all the teasing at school, particularly from the boys, I was not very confident around men and liked to keep them at arm's length. Growing up as a teenager I never felt like I fitted in with all my friends who were so concerned about make-up, hair and getting a boyfriend. But during this time of healing, and as I began to feel comfortable with being a woman and being feminine, I noticed men were beginning to be attracted to me. I had always felt so ugly and I am sure guys had picked up on that but now I could see men were actually noticing me and beginning to give me compliments. It felt good!

My Father takes me shopping

Something most girls love is to be taken shopping. One day, when I was having a prayer time, I felt God say to me: 'I want to take you shopping!' A few hours later someone came and gave me some money saying: 'God told me to give you this.' I knew it was money to go shopping with! So I went into town – just God and me. I felt really excited, like I was being taken out on a day trip with my dad! I needed to get some new pyjamas so I asked him to help me choose. I went into one shop and there in the middle of a huge rack of pyjamas was a soft cuddly blue pair with a huge red heart on the front. As soon as I saw them I felt God say to me, 'Those are the ones, and every time you put them on I want you to remember how much I love you.' I nearly started to cry right there in the shop.

Soon after that I went on a trip to speak in a church and after the meeting a man came up to me and said, 'Here's some money. God says, go shopping!'

Another time I was on a trip to Florida and the lady I was staying with commented on my clothes not being very feminine; that women of God needed to dress appropriately – and tomorrow she was taking me shopping! The next day I was taken to a very nice mall and bought two new outfits. I couldn't believe it. As soon as I opened the door to God fathering me, he really did step in and father me in ways I never expected.

Facing fears

Expect the Lord to walk you through, and out of, your fears. For people with eating disorders a real fear is food. For those with anorexia it is the fear of getting fat. For those with food addiction it is the fear of not having food. A huge fear of mine was fasting. I hated the feeling of being empty and would feel panicky at the thought of not having food.

A few of my friends had successfully finished a forty-day fast and had experienced real breakthrough in intimacy with God; I, on the other hand, had struggled – my fast lasted two days! I felt like such a failure and couldn't understand why food still had such a hold on me.

I was part of a leadership team who were going on an outreach to Costa Rica. We had decided to fast for twenty-one days – just fruit and vegetables. Two days into the fast I was invited to a church with a few friends to help pray for people. I accepted the offer and set off for a weekend away leaving the rest of the team eating veggies and fruit. On the way to the church my friends stopped at a well-known fast food place! First temptation! But after some careful thought I convinced myself that fries were technically a vegetable and therefore I was allowed fries. When we arrived at the church, all the ladies had got together to

Romans 8:39: Nothing can separate me (not even my faults) from God's Love for me.

make a huge meal . . . and I could only eat a few green beans! By the evening I was starving and we all went to the local shop for some snacks. I managed to again convince myself and my friends that crisps were technically a vegetable and therefore crisps were allowed. So I bought a huge packet of crisps. But as I was busy licking my fingers and finishing off the last few crumbs, I began to feel so guilty. There I was, leader of the team, cheating while all the students were faithfully eating yet more veggies for tea!

I remember going to my room and writing in my journal, 'I am useless, God. How can you love me? I can't even fast two days for you!'

Then God started to speak to me, so I wrote down what I felt he was saying. (The reason I am sharing this is to bring some comfort to those of you who feel you fail time and time again and will never get free of this.)

He said, 'Food has been your comfort, your closest friend in the hardest times of your life. But now you have chosen me to be your comfort. When a child has breast-fed for months, the mother slowly weans her child off her breast and on to solid food. But she does it gradually, step by step, day by day. Otherwise the child feels insecure, robbed and afraid. The mother holds her child; the child rejects the new food, spitting it out, wanting the old way of life-support where the child knows that nourishment can be found. But the mother continues to feed the child little by little, until the child accepts the new food.

'Like this mother, Maxine, I am slowly weaning you off milk and on to food, taking you from your old ways to your new ways. But it's me doing it – just as it is not the baby's responsibility but the mother's. I am your mother as well as your Father. I will tend to you. I know when it is time to introduce solid food. You are my child, my

*Jeremiah 31:3: Father Loves me with an everlasting love.
I have never not been loved by my Father.*

responsibility. Let me parent you. Does the child tell the mother how to train her? No.'

I had expected him to say, 'Yup, you're right, you can't even fast for me. Just shows where you're at.'

A lot of people who struggle with food problems have that sort of expectancy and shame because they've tried and tried, again and again. I needed to learn to let go and say, 'God, I can't do it, but you have promised to fill this void in my heart. You have promised to put yourself in the place of food. You have promised to do that.'

Fear of hunger

You see I had a fear of feeling empty, of being hungry. But the Lord was saying, 'Face your fear with me, and I will walk with you through it. But you need to experience and know that I am enough for you. Face your fear with me!'

So I told him I'd fast for one day. Through the day, I just asked the Lord for help when I was feeling hungry. And I did it. I survived.

Then when I woke up the next day, I asked the Lord again for grace, just one more day's worth of strength. And as we walked through that second day I became really, really hungry and I felt this fear rising inside of me. 'Lord, I'm feeling fearful. I want to eat right now, but you say in your word that you are enough for me, and I want you to prove that to me.'

On the third day I was scheduled to preach and minister in a class and I expected to wind up as a mess on the floor with low blood sugar and dizziness and whatever! But actually I felt stronger than I did when I was eating. And when I finished the three-day fast, I not only felt like I'd accomplished something significant and new, it also broke my fear of hunger – and God demonstrated that he could see me through.

John 14:23: Father likes being with me so much that He made His home within me.

> *A cautionary note: I do not recommend fasting from food as a way to conquer eating problems or as a self-test of how healed you are. In fact, I wouldn't do it until you are way on the other side of being healed. The physical sensations and physiological changes during a fast are just too reminiscent of what you experience while struggling with anorexia or bulimia or failed diets. It could set you back seriously.*

There are lots of other things you can fast from if you are looking for ways to cultivate spiritual discipline or if you want to heighten your prayer life – try fasting from TV, or newspapers and magazines, computer time, your car, make-up, 'label' clothing, music. Or perhaps favourite food luxuries, like sugar, spices, caffeine, or alcohol. If you think the Lord is suggesting a fast from food, make sure you first submit the idea to someone who can speak into your life with authority (i.e. say, 'Wait' or 'No'!) like a pastor or house group leader. Make sure they are fully aware of your background regarding eating patterns!

Learning how to eat again

When I had bulimia, I had no discipline – my inner strength was shattered and I had no self-worth to re-build it. In contrast, an anorexic person is off at the other end of the scale, exercising an enormous amount of self-discipline that has become self-consuming. What God wants for us is a loving, helpful self-discipline that strengthens us and brings us closer to him: A healthy inner strength, which comes from him, not our own domineering self-will.

An alcoholic can stop drinking alcohol, a drug addict can stop taking drugs, but for someone recovering

Relax – He loves you!

from an eating disorder – you can't simply stop eating! You have to learn how to eat again. Through the years of bulimia my stomach was very messed up. When I ate I always felt sick, bloated and often had stomach cramps. I had no idea when I was hungry or when I was full; when I started to eat I didn't know when to stop. I was used to being able to eat lots of food and not put weight on. I really needed help as to how to eat normally again.

I asked God my Father to help me. Now, I wasn't quite prepared for what he asked me to do. The Lord was about to put me on his very own nutritional programme!

The Lord told me, 'This is a season of discipline for you, Maxine,' and he told me to cut out sugar, refined flour (white bread, pasta, etc.) and alcohol. 'Stop eating those for a year. If you stop eating those for a year, in this discipline I will heal you.' When I first heard this I thought this cannot be God, there is no way I could give up all those things for a year – especially not sugar! So I asked him to confirm this to me in two different ways. He did through my mum and a close friend, who very quickly confirmed they definitely thought this was God speaking.

The year began and I thought I would never make it. I felt grumpy and depressed without these foods and could not imagine that life was worth living without them. Many times I wanted to give up and if it hadn't been for my close friend, Shelley, encouraging me and praying for me I would have. As time went on it got easier and I stopped craving sugar; I realised that these were the foods I was addicted to. These are the foods that numb us and suppress pain – the foods I had turned to when I was feeling low.

'Because you are sons, God sent the Sprit of his Son into our heart, the Spirit who calls out, "Abba, Father." So you are no longer a slave, but a son; and since you are a son, God has made you also an heir.' (Galatians 4:6,7 – NIV)

Let him comfort you

God says he wants to be our comfort, he wants to be the one who is there for us, but too often we turn to the fridge or to the TV or to a friend before we go to him. During this year I realised just how much I depended on food to make me feel better rather than on God. I was angry that I couldn't eat whatever I liked, I was angry that God wouldn't just heal me, and make my stomach better so I could enjoy food again.

I used to keep a journal where I would write down my thoughts to God. One time I was having a particularly bad day and I wrote: 'Lord, I'm so angry with you. I have pleaded with you to heal me and still I'm ill. Why haven't you healed me? I've tried everything . . . I've asked people to pray for me for healing, I have eaten well, and I have believed that you want to heal me Why am I not well?'

Then I heard a quiet response: 'Everything but ME. You never came to ME.'

My response: 'But Lord, what do you mean? I've asked you night after night to heal me. But no, I wake up the next day, feeling ill again.'

Then I kept hearing repeatedly: 'You haven't really come to ME. You never came to ME. You've shouted at me, tried to manipulate me by bargaining for your health, but have you really come to ME?'

'Lord, I don't understand!'

Then I saw a picture of a little girl who had hurt her knee and was running crying to her dad. Her father picked her up in his arms and kissed her knee better. She jumped down and ran away to play – happy again. You know how kids are – the pain hasn't actually changed but it was the kiss from Dad that made it all better!

Then God said this to me: 'Lord, Lord, you call me Lord, but I want to be your daddy, the one to kiss your knee and make it all better. I want to be the one my little girl looks at and knows it was her daddy that made it all better. That one kiss from her daddy made all the pain go away and made her smile again. I want to be that for you. Not the doctors, a diet, family or friends, but ME – I AM YOUR DAD!'

As God spoke to me I had a revelation: I didn't know how to go to God for him to comfort me. I was used to comforting myself. My own dad had never kissed my knee and made it all better. I don't remember him wiping away any of my tears. I had no concept of a God of comfort. My comfort had been a big tub of ice cream. After this revelation I realised God wanted me to come to him. Now I am learning to turn to my heavenly Father when I am feeling lonely, or frustrated, or anxious. I usually put on some music and just listen to the words and let the Holy Spirit come and comfort me. It sounds very simple but when I do this I can feel him lift off my worries and leave me with a peace again.

For me, changing my eating habits hasn't been automatic, or easy, or fun (and certainly not convenient), but step by step, little by little, I have been set free from the control food had over me. I had spent many years forming bad eating habits and now I am re-learning new healthy patterns. There are so many diets out there but if you simply cut down on foods full of sugar, stay off refined carbohydrates and eat plenty of fruit and vegetables you will find your cravings stop and you naturally stay at the weight God designed for your body. (Of course, I am talking generally – I am aware that some people have medical problems which affect their weight.) I have read a lot about nutrition and healthy eating and personally try to stick to the diet God gave me. In the beginning I was very strict with my eating but now I find I can have treats and still not start binge eating. It is possible for your tastes to change and to actually enjoy a life of carrot juice and lentil casseroles!

Keep a diary

I suggest you give this a try! Buy yourself a diary where you write down your thoughts to God: the good, bad and the ugly! I encourage you to be real with your Father. When you have finished writing, note what you feel he is saying to you. It may be a word, a sentence or a picture but I assure you your Father has a lot that he wants to say to you if you give him a chance. If you are not sure that what you have written down is from God, then show a friend and see what they think. Here's a tip: if it is something that encourages you then that is probably from God but if it is something that condemns you and brings you down then it is not from your Father.

Lifting off shame

I want to share one other important thing with you before I take you through some prayers and practical advice. I believe you'll find this helpful in healing eating disorders.

It's about the secrecy and shame. What you've been doing may be embarrassing and difficult to admit; it may make you feel dirty, or ugly, or like a hopeless failure; it may be an unshakeable sadness that you've resigned yourself to; or it may leave you feeling like an outsider that no one can understand. That is the grip of shame.

Part of the reason shame has such a hold is that you can actually see how you deserve those feelings – at least it

Freedom is knowing you are loved.

seems that way, because deep down you know something's wrong. And it isn't just what you're doing; you assume it's all because there's something wrong with you. And since you have a good sense of what is and isn't fair, you're simply being fair about yourself. You believe it, you deserve it, and you own it. That is shame.

But think about this: everyone has made the same sorts of mistakes, been hurt in similar ways, yet the people around you don't struggle the way you do. They're free, and you're not. That is shame.

Let me tell you how Jesus broke my shame.

I was once having a prayer time and I suddenly had this mental picture of myself in the bathroom in Sweden where I used to make myself sick. And I had this terrible thought: 'Jesus is in here with me! Oh Lord, anywhere but here! You can meet me anywhere but here. This is the place where I get rid of everything that is horrible in me.' This was the horrible time. 'Please don't meet me in here.'

But there he was, standing in front of me. He simply reached over and wiped away some of the sick from my face, and I just broke down in tears. I said to the Lord, 'Don't meet me here, not here, not in my shame. Let me tidy myself up. Don't see me like this.' But I sensed the Lord saying, 'This is where I want to meet you. This is the place. I want to touch the place where there is shame, the place where there is hurt, the place where there is pain. Let me go back to that place. That is where I will meet you, not when you've pulled it all together.'

The picture he showed me was simple and all he did was touch my face and wipe away the sick. But the impact it had on my heart changed me forever. You see this was a side of me I didn't let anyone see. This was the side of me that was dirty, shameful and desperate. This was the part of me I kept hidden from my family and friends. But this was the part of me the Lord wanted to touch. When he looked at me with eyes full of love I knew he loved the whole of me . . . that there was nothing I could hide from him.

You may find that you need to let him meet you in the most painful, shameful place. I was praying for a friend of mine who had suffered sexual abuse and as we prayed together she just kept saying, 'I feel so dirty.' I asked God to come and speak to her. As I waited quietly she began to cry, but then her tears turned to laughter. God had showed her a picture of herself in a changing room; she had been standing there, alone, wearing horrible, dirty underwear, then God gave her some beautiful new white underwear to put on and told her she was clean and beautiful. When she shared this story with me I started to cry too. God is so personal and knows exactly how and where to meet each one of us.

In the seven years that I have been praying for people I have heard many stories like this – of how God has met people in such an intimate way and spoken things to them that have changed the way they see themselves.

Happy ending

I am thirty-one now, and feel like my eating disorder is a distant memory. God really has restored everything to me that the enemy had stolen. Today I have a very good relationship with both my mum and my dad; I have friends who know and love me just the way I am. I am able to live a healthy and happy life and have even met someone very special whom I am hoping to marry next year. I hope that my testimony will give you hope that you are not alone; with God as your Father, he can and will put all the pieces of your life back together.

Now I know that He loves me just the way I am.

8

Prayer Ministry

*I*f you struggle with anorexia or bulimia or compulsive eating, then you may already be in the place where you can't help yourself – but the Lord can help you, and he's willing. So here's the decision you have to make: Have you had enough yet? Will you let him in to the roots of your struggle? Remember, he wants change, not just relieve (though he may let you have a break before delving into the root issues!).

Break the secrecy

If your pattern is still secret, then you need to break the secrecy and tell someone what's going on. And it might not be the easiest person to tell – telling my mum, and then my church, was very humbling but I had come to a place where I was willing to break through the fear of embarrassment. Don't just tell a friend that you don't have to listen to; when I first tried to tell my sister she just said, 'Well, if it helps you get thin, why not!' Tell someone who has a position of authority in your life and ask him or her to pray. Make sure they pray *with* you and not just *for* you.

Why don't we pray now?

When I'm sharing my story in a church setting, there's always a time of prayer, but there's no reason why that can't happen now as you read this book. It's more important that you and God get together about this than you and me! One-on-one prayer is often preferable, but people have come to me after a whole congregation prayed together, and said: 'God is setting me free! Something really changed. It really did change, and there is hope. There is hope!'

Meet the healer

If you don't know God the way I've been talking about him, as a loving Father, or as Jesus who lived with us as God 'in person', or the Holy Spirit who is God's tangible presence here and now, why don't you give him the opportunity to show you what he's actually like?

Do you know that Jesus, God's own Son came and lived a perfect life here on earth, and then laid that life down for you? When he died on the cross, he took the punishment for all the sins you (and I) have ever done. He did this so that we could be free! What does that mean? It means we have no righteousness or holiness of our own, but Jesus did a kind of magnificent swap. He took our bad things, and he gives us his own righteousness. You can be friends with God and live with him forever – not because of anything you have done to 'make you right with him', but because Jesus has made it possible. Read John 3:16 and 1 Corinthians 1:30. You might want to say this prayer before you read on:

Remember, he designed you, he loves you, and he wants to heal you!

Heavenly Father, I have rebelled against you. I have sinned in my thoughts, my words and my actions, sometimes unconsciously, sometimes deliberately. I am sorry for the way I have lived and I ask you to forgive me. Thank you that Jesus died on the cross so that I could be forgiven. Lord, I ask you to reveal your Son to me now. Please send your Holy Spirit to help me follow him whatever the cost. Amen.

Remember, he designed you, he loves you, and he wants to heal you! Here's another prayer.

> Jesus, I don't know you this way, but if you really want to show me, then I really want to know you. It seems I can't help myself, so would you please help me with these problems? I choose to begin trusting you.

OK, let's see what he does!

Healing prayers

I'll pray, and you can just agree with me.

> Holy Spirit, would you come now? I ask you to come and search this heart. I ask that you would reveal the roots, the root causes of this struggle. If there were things that were said, hurtful words, bad decisions, or lies believed, what do you want to reveal about them? Where did the self-rejection come in, Lord? Where did this hidden hunger come from?

Now you can expect the Lord to start answering, immediately or over time, by reminding you of things: people, places, events etc. Sometimes it will be a name or some other clue. Just keep asking where it's leading and I'm sure you'll get there!

I've found the following prayer to be very effective. It may overlap a little in places, but it covers a lot. The effect may be immediate or it may be more gradual, but I believe you will start to see and feel change. And it doesn't have to be a once-only thing: it might be a good idea to go through it again in a few days or weeks when you feel the need. A girl contacted me and said she had been to one of my teaching seminars and had taken a copy of the prayer. She didn't think it would really help as she had suffered from bulimia for years; she'd been in and out of hospital but nothing had worked. But she was so excited to tell me that each day she read through this prayer – and it was working! She hadn't made herself sick and could really feel a change was happening.

Pray:

Father, help me to understand that you made me a beautiful person in which your Spirit can live; that my body is a temple of the Holy Spirit.

I know I have overloaded and abused my body by requiring it to constantly digest food, or forcing it to reject food, or by withholding food when I was hungry.

I have allowed myself to be both the abuser and the abused.

Father, forgive me for not taking care of my body and give me the grace to eat healthily.

I bind my spirit, soul and body to your will, confessing that I have not been doing what is best for me.

I loose myself from all wrong attitudes about food.

I loose wrong emotional reactions that I have used as an excuse for eating comfort foods.

I repent of using food to stuff my body in order to dull my sensations when I feel pain inside.

I repent of pushing myself by starving my body when I am dealing with pain.

I choose to separate the needs of the normal physical function of my body from the unnatural neediness of my soul (my will and emotions).

Jesus, please come: heal my emotions, my wounds, and fill the voids in my soul with your love.

I give you the inward parts of my body to your will and purpose. My throat, stomach and digestive system, my heart, liver, colon, circulatory system, brain, nervous system, as well as everything else you have created within me.

Jesus, I ask you now to come and heal my physical body.

Through practising an eating disorder, you have probably altered your own body chemistry, damaged some parts, overridden natural processes and cycles

Physical, chemical change

Through practising an eating disorder, you have probably altered your own body chemistry, damaged some parts, overridden natural processes and cycles; so let me pray about that now.

Where there is a chemical imbalance, where there is an addiction to food, where the original plan for this body has been tampered with and interrupted, I ask you, Holy Spirit, to come and heal it now in the authority of Jesus' name. Come and heal this physical body, re-start the natural processes that have been shut down, strengthen what has been intentionally weakened.

If you've experienced those feelings of being out of control as you've struggled, we need to take down some strongholds of belief. So pray with me.

Father, I repent for accepting lies about myself as truth. I ask you to forgive me for rejecting myself. I also repent for comparing myself to the images that the media and other people hold up as 'beauty', and for constantly thinking negative thoughts about myself. I choose to believe the truth about how you see me, Jesus: that you see beauty in me. Teach me to see myself through your eyes.

I repent for using food to medicate and even drug myself when the pain of unhealed hurts seems too much. Help me to seek you, Jesus, as the spiritual bread of life that will bring me freedom, healing, joy and peace.

Lord, I repent for controlling my life with food and for not trusting you. I give over control to you, my loving Father.

A bit of housecleaning!

I know the Lord wants to do a deep healing, and I know from personal experience that your physical struggles have been driven by self-destructive thought patterns, perhaps even seeming like 'voices' in your head. I hope you can handle this, but in addition to the physical and mental aspects there's probably also a spiritual dimension to your struggle which has been aggravated by the presence of, let's call them 'spiritual squatters'. By that I mean unhealthy spirits who, like vagrants, occupy land or buildings they don't rightly own. These are spirits characterised by and associated with anorexia, bulimia and compulsive over-eating (the old-fashioned word is 'gluttony') that exert their influence when the conditions are favourable i.e. when we've given them credence and even control by buying into their arguments and practising their ways.

By our bad choices and using (or not using) our wills, we've permitted them squatters' rights. But we can renounce them, take back what they've taken and give the keys back to God. If you're willing to make that change, then just tell the Lord, 'OK,' and I'll pray for you now.

In the authority and under the name of Jesus, I take authority over those spiritual squatters and I break the spiritual grip of anorexia, bulimia, compulsive eating and self-hatred. With the power of the spoken word, I break their hold on your mind and body. I command silence to those constant thoughts of self-hatred and I speak peace to that battle in your mind. I command a halt to the spiritual harassment and intimidation.

I also take authority over every negative thought pattern. I exert Jesus' authority over them now and loosen their grip. Holy Spirit, every place that this mind has been attacked, in every way that this person has believed all those lies about themselves, I ask you to come and break the power of those lies now.

I take authority over every negative word that has been spoken over you, every horrible name that you have been called, and the way these spoken things have become self-fulfilling curses over your life. I break the power of those words – the weight of them comes off your thinking now, off your body's responses to those directives, and I break the influence of those spirits off your personal spirit.

I break the hold of those compulsions – anorexia, bulimia, gluttony and self-hatred – even now those voices must flee at the sound of Jesus' name.

Now you may have felt something dramatic happen – or it may have been subtle, you may not have noticed anything yet! But just as words have had a disastrous, harmful impact on you, I believe these prayers will bring life, healing and freedom to you. Your choosing to agree with them will give them weight and influence.

Forgiveness

Now, or perhaps later, you may find yourself thinking of people that you need to forgive. Choose to forgive them for the things they've said and done (or not said and done) and the effects they've had on you in your struggle with eating patterns. I'll leave it to you to pray through that forgiveness, but remember: the more freedom you give, the more you gain!

9

Some Practical Advice

Keep short accounts

- A great idea is to have an accountability partner, someone you can be open and honest with. Someone who will ask you from time to time: 'Hey, how's it going?' and be there for you when you are having a bad day;
- Be honest with yourself and others when you are struggling. Don't be tempted to do this alone;
- Ask for help. As long as you keep it in the dark the enemy can really take advantage and blow things out of proportion.

Keep a food diary

God challenged me to keep a food diary and to write down everything I had eaten that day, and then in the evenings before I went to bed we would go through it together.

The reason this really helped me was because when I had bulimia I had been eating vast amounts of food and had no idea what a normal portion size was or even when I was full. When I wrote what I had eaten that day I could see when I was eating too much or not enough.

Going through this each day with God really helped me in my recovery. He comforted me when I was down and encouraged me when I was doing well.

Write a diary

Try writing out your thoughts to God. Each day just take ten minutes to write down what is on your heart and then wait and give God a chance to tell you his thoughts.

Stay off foods you are addicted to

As I mentioned earlier we can get addicted to certain kinds of foods. For me it was sugar. As soon as I ate something sweet I found it very hard to stop eating. It would often trigger a craving but I found I didn't get those cravings when I kept off sugar. It can be the same with carbohydrates for some people. Learn to listen to your body and stay away from the foods that trigger the cravings.

Get busy

When you are struggling with an eating disorder it can tend to take over your whole life. I suggest you start some new activities to keep you busy and take your attention off yourself and off food.

Stop and think for a moment of something you

Next time you are feeling down, instead of reaching for the biscuit tin, call a friend or go and spend some time with God have always wanted to do. For example, I always wanted to do photography so I decided to buy myself a camera and join a course. Maybe you have always wanted to sing. Well, why not take a few lessons or take up an instrument? God put those desires in your heart for a reason.

Start to care for yourself

Next time you are feeling down, instead of reaching for the biscuit tin, call a friend or go and spend some time with God. You need to change your old patterns for new ones. As you begin to love yourself again you will naturally want to take care of your body and the way you eat.

Speak positively

Speak words of encouragement over yourself instead of words that bring you down. Sometimes we are our own worst enemy. Be nice to yourself!

Stay close to God

He really is the one to lean on and to cry out to when things are difficult.

If you are not already part of a church I suggest you join one! This way you will learn more about him and also have the encouragement of friends who know him.

Some advice for family and friends

If you suspect that a family member or friend is struggling with an eating disorder encourage them to talk to you about it.

- See if they are open to seeking professional advice.
- It is important that you listen to the person, be supportive and caring.
- Don't give advice until they ask for it.
- Realise that the person will not change until they want to.
- Try not to nag, threaten or manipulate as this will not make any difference.
- Never criticize or shame – the person already feels guilty enough.
- Don't waste time trying to convince the person to eat or stop eating so much.
- Don't say, 'You are too thin' – this will encourage her to continue dieting.
- Don't say, 'It is good you have gained weight' – she will then try to lose it.
- Do activities that take the person's mind of the disorder.
- Try not to talk about food and weight all the time.
- Do show a lot of love and speak encouraging words about how special they are.

Useful contact information

For further information about eating disorders, contact your GP or any of the following recommended organisations.

Kainos Trust is committed to helping people to reach and sustain full recovery from eating disorders through practical teaching, Christian principles and personal support.
The Lower George House
High Street
Newnham-on-Severn
Gloucestershire
GL14 1BS
Telephone: 01594 516284
Fax: 01594 516704
Email enquiries@kainostrust.co.uk
Registered Charity No:1058040 – Director: Helena Wilkinson

Eating Disorder Association (EDA)
1st Floor, Wensum House
103 Prince of Wales Road
Norwich
Norfolk
NR1 1DW
Adult Helpline: 01603 621414, Monday–Friday 09:00–18:30
Youth Helpline: 01603 765050, Monday–Friday 16:00–18:30
Recorded information line: 0906 302 0012 (50p per minute)

Centre for Eating Disorders (Scotland)
3 Sciences Road
Edinburgh,
EH9 1LE
Scotland
Tel: 0131 668 3051 Answerphone out of hours
Open: Monday–Friday 09:00–19:00 – appointments only
This is an independent organisation giving cover to Scotland. They offer psychotherapy aimed at helping people to change eating behaviours and self-denigrating attitudes.

National Centre for Eating Disorders
54 New Road
Surrey
KT10 9NU
Tel: 01372 469493 Answerphone out of hours
Open: Monday–Friday 10:00–13:00
This is not a charity. It has national cover and aims to treat compulsive eating, anorexia, bulimia and weight problems by means of support, prevention and training. They have professional staff giving advice to callers. They will dispatch information free of charge upon request to anyone who may be concerned with an eating disorder.

Anorexia and Bulimia Care
15 Fernhurst Gate
Aughton
Ormskirk
Lancashire
L39 5ED
Tel: 01695 422479
This national organisation supports sufferers and their carers of anorexia, bulimia and compulsive eating disorders. They can point people towards support groups or put people in touch with ex-sufferers.

Overeaters Anonymous
PO Box 19
Stretford
Manchester
M32 9EB
Tel: 07000 784985 (24-hour)
This is a registered charity giving national cover. They are a self-help group aimed at those people whose lives have been affected by compulsive behaviour around food e.g. overeating, anorexia, and bulimia.

10

Testimonies

Caroline Bone
I started to struggle with an eating disorder when I was in my mid-twenties. My parents divorced when I was nineteen and my father died a few years later. Pressures at work and home were growing and I felt like food was my only comfort and friend. I would eating large quantities of food at one time and keep food hidden away in my room. Later, though, I began to panic about putting on weight and would try to make myself sick – fortunately I did not succeed and consequently concluded I did not have a problem. I was in denial.

About four years later, whilst living in Canada, attending the School of Ministry, I was in the café one day and bought some sweets. I quickly put them into my pocket so that no one else would see. As I did, I felt the Holy Spirit stop me in my tracks, saying: 'What are you doing?' I could deny it no longer – food had a hold on my life. I spoke with one of the staff and they prayed for me and I agreed to be accountable to them. I realised that I was allowing food to be my comforter rather than God.

Over the previous months God had been teaching me what it meant to be fathered by him and how little I understood about what that meant because, like most fathers, mine wasn't perfect. One particular area I struggled with was trying to live up to my father's expectations and constantly feeling like I failed. My dad found it very difficult to show me his love, which also added to my feelings of worthlessness.

I had to deal with these and many other issues in my life, learning to forgive those who had hurt me and repent of my own sinful actions. As I did this more and more I was able to know God's love for me and feel secure in that love. The food issue was out in the open but I had my good days and my bad days and I still didn't feel in control. Finally the day came when I had had enough and I told God I was willing to give up my right to use food as a comfort, asking him to set me free. The two people who were with me when I came to this point prayed for me and I was set free from a spirit of addiction.

Now I was free to choose the way I used food – but I emphasise 'choose'. I felt very different after that prayer but times of testing still came. When my world was shaken by circumstances outside my control I had to choose to ask God to help me and allow him to be my comfort instead of food. The more I did this the more I found that God was a far better comforter!

Michelle Kowalczyk (*Maxine's older sister*)
I am thirty-four years old, happily married and have two children. When I was eighteen, studying for a degree in Art and Design at Winchester, I fell into a trap of feeling fat and ugly. Everyone around me seemed to be so much slimmer and more attractive so I decided to put myself on a diet. It started with a diet but before long I wasn't really eating much at all and whatever I did eat was high in fibre so it would go through me

quickly. Some days all I would eat would be one apple and then, just to lose more weight, I would go swimming at lunch times. I also started using laxatives to lose weight quickly.

Visits home to my family were difficult as they were starting to notice all the weight I had lost. I used to dread meal times. Eventually my boyfriend (now husband) told my parents he was concerned as I wasn't eating. My father was very angry and threatened to stop helping financially towards my course if I didn't start eating. I remember I was really resentful towards him and just blocked my family out, focusing more on myself. My struggle with food went on for years. It wasn't until I was married and fell pregnant with our first child that I had to begin to eat properly. I remember resenting having to eat, though, and did not put on very much weight at all. It wasn't until a visiting speaker came to our church and spoke about eating disorders that I realised I had anorexia. That day I got some prayer and cried a lot. I realised what a hold the enemy had over my life. Every day I was controlled with thoughts about food and getting thin; I was never satisfied with my body. God was telling me I needed to learn to love myself and to daily reject the lies of the enemy. I had to tell myself I was beautiful and special and that I had a beautiful body. My husband had been telling me this for years but I could not receive it.

Through asking for help and letting God heal my heart I can now hear my heavenly Father tell me that he is crazy about me just the way I am, that I don't have to try to change for him – he loves me just the way I am!

Today I don't think about dieting – people comment, 'How do you stay so lovely and thin?' I say things like, 'Oh, you know, mother of two always rushing around!' but that is not entirely true. I have surrendered dieting and slimming to God and that was hard because I had to let go. I had to not be in control; that is hard for me because I feel more safe and secure when I am calling all the shots! But I had a choice and I chose to let go and God has been so close to me through it. He told me he would help me through my anorexia and I trusted him and now I can sit down and enjoy a healthy meal with my family. I am a wife and a mum but firstly I am a child of God. My value does not depend on my performance or other people's opinions of me. My identity is in being his child.

Wendy (a qualified doctor who is now training as a Christian counsellor)
I was fifteen when I developed anorexia (which six months later became bulimia). So by the time I stood on the brink of the long bumpy road to recovery in my late thirties, I had lived longer with an eating disorder than without one! It felt like a huge risk. Questions bombarded my mind: 'How will I do this? How can I cope without my eating disorder? How will I live a normal adult life when I've never done that before? What is normal anyway?' Life was hell, and getting more unstable, but better the devil you know? A quiet voice beckoned: 'I have come that you might have life, and life to the full – more abundantly.' Did I have that? Emphatically no! I was ashamed of my quality of life as a Christian of many years. What kind of a witness was I? I had tasted the deeper and richer things of God and wanted more. But there was this slight obstacle!

I was encouraged by the biblical account of the man who has been ill for thirty-eight years; he was healed so it wasn't too late for me. But I had to answer the question Jesus asked him: 'Do you want to get well?' For so long my answer had been, 'On balance, no thanks.' Now, approaching forty, with the eating disorder getting more and more out of control, wondering whether I'd ever be what God intended, how could I look him in the eye and see all that might have been? I was haunted by the thought of Judgement Day and the bitter regrets. The balance was tipped and I said yes.

What God showed me in the months that followed, through a Bible study in the Song of Solomon, gave me the biggest shock of my life and turned all my years of guilt and shame upside-down. He revealed his grace in a very deep way. I came to see that I am loved, enjoyed, and delighted in by God. More than that: the basis for this extravagant love is the sacrifice of Jesus on the cross. Nothing I do or don't do affects how much he loves me. As I stood looking at the tatters of my life, I heard God say: 'Even if you never get better, I will love and delight in you just as much. That's not my best for you, but know this – I will feel the same about you whatever happens in the future.'

I look back on this as the foundation for my journey to where I am today. It took the 'pressure to perform' completely away. It poured balm into my broken, enslaved heart. It stripped off my garments of shame. The affirming, encouraging, uplifting things I read in that wonderful portion of God's word, made real to my heart by the Holy Spirit, changed my view of myself. I'd always had low self-esteem and filtered the teaching on Christian humility through that. I thought the world would be a better place without me, that I was a nobody, a failure, an embarrassment to God. Sure, he loved me, but I saw it as more of a general benevolent tolerance than a passionate, focused, intimate emotion directed at me personally. Now I was discovering the intoxicating truth that I am the cherished bride and chosen eternal companion of Jesus

Christ himself; that his heart beats for me, even skips a beat when I look at him! With this backdrop I could dare to look at all the painful, shameful, even sinful issues lurking inside me that had led to my eating disorder. Nothing I was about to uncover would deter my heavenly lover. I could look God in the eye, naked yet not ashamed. I had hidden for so long. Now I was learning to run to him, instead of from him, with what was broken. I had a new identity – not 'anorexic' or 'bulimic' but God's beloved. I had significance and security. The road was still going to be long and hard but hearing him call forth my beauty made it bearable. Knowing he was going to finish what he had begun gave me courage and hope. His words of truth and freedom have been my stepping stones over the tumultuous sea of lies, torment and bondage. There is nothing more deeply satisfying than to experience passionate affection from God. It's what we're made for!

*L*aurie Ross

I went through a period of depression when I was in my latter teens and early twenties, and during that time I began to realize that the one thing I could control in life and that gave me a sense of accomplishment, something I desperately needed to feel at the time, was my intake of food. But I'm getting ahead of myself, so let me take you further back in time to when I was in my early teens, still in high school, and feeling very alone and unprotected. Then I used food as a comfort when I got home from school – and I mean as soon as I got home. I almost ran to the kitchen cupboard, grabbed a big bag of chips, went to my room, shut the door and wolfed my chips down as I read some mediocre book to escape the incredibly deep pain I felt. That was my routine, for maybe three years, until I bottomed out at the beginning of twelfth grade, when I broke down and just couldn't face going back to school another day.

So I dropped out, not only of school but also of going to church, and refused to see any of my friends. Thank God I had a loving and supportive family behind me at that time, because I don't know what I would have done without them! Anyway, I started to notice the change in the way I viewed food when I was nineteen and I started to exercise. I also found I could eat less, and that gave me a tremendous sense of pride and accomplishment because it seemed everyone else around me was struggling in that area but I wasn't! I would hear people talk about Christmas and the dread I would hear in their voices because they knew, inevitably, despite their good intentions, they would put on more weight and be carrying Christmas with them into the new year. I didn't understand why they couldn't exert the same willpower that was second nature to me. How deceived I was!

It became harder and harder to live this life of obsessive rigidity and I was getting more and more terrified of getting fat. It got to the point where if butter touched my food I would have to make up for it by exercising the next day, even if I felt like collapsing from exhaustion because I didn't have enough fuel in my poor little body to support that kind of exertion, or even just to get me through the day. I was seeing a doctor for regular check-ups and she just happened to be a Christian. Well actually I think my friend and counsellor at the time recommended her to me and I am sure it was totally set up by God. I wasn't only getting counselling to deal with the food disorder but for depression as well. My doctor was counselling me and I was also receiving counselling through my church, but God was only getting started! At one point I was almost sent to the hospital because I was still losing weight, but that obviously wasn't part of God's plan because it never happened! Yeah God!

My doctor referred me to a professional counsellor who specialized in working with people who have eating disorders and the decision was made to go and see her. I think God was slightly more determined to see me well than I was, because he set up just the right network of divinely appointed human resources to be at my disposal and to give me the push I needed in the right direction. And they made sure I was accountable, but in such a loving way. They all knew I wouldn't get better until I decided to and it wasn't easy, to say the least, because I had been under the control of the eating disorder, which I named 'Shoo Fly', for approximately three years. But I decided to trust what other people were telling me, even though the lies in my head were screaming the opposite. I allowed God to take over little by little by surrendering my so-called 'control' over to his perfect control, because he knew what was best, even when I couldn't see it literally with my own eyes. I couldn't trust my eyes or my ears, so I had to lean on his and those he used to help me see the truth.

The problem wasn't solved overnight and I faced days and moments of panic when I ate something I would never have allowed myself to eat before, but I slowly began to realize that I wasn't going to go completely berserk and eat everything in sight – which is what my worst fear had been in deciding to get better. It took me a while to find the right balance and a body weight that was comfortable, but God was so faithful, especially when the pendulum was swinging in the opposite direction, as it naturally does when you've restricted yourself like that for so long – but I never got fat. I had to learn to trust the one who made my body and allow him to heal the pain and the source of the eating disorder that started long before the symptoms began: when I had felt so unprotected and believed that God wouldn't be there for me, so I had to be in control. He then became a comfort that stuck to my bones and really nourished me for the first time. Plus, I was able to enjoy eating again. And now there's nothing I won't eat as long as I'm getting a good balance!

How Do I See Myself?

Father, How Do You See Me?
